THE HISTORY

OF

No. 31 SQUADRON

ROYAL FLYING CORPS

AND

ROYAL AIR FORCE

in the East
from its formation in 1915 to 1950

The Naval & Military Press Ltd

in association with

The Imperial War Museum
Department of Printed Books

Published jointly by
The Naval & Military Press Ltd
Unit 10 Ridgewood Industrial Park,
Uckfield, East Sussex,
TN22 5QE England
Tel: +44 (0) 1825 749494
Fax: +44 (0) 1825 765701
www.naval–military-press.com

and

The Imperial War Museum, London
Department of Printed Books
www.iwm.org.uk

THE HISTORY OF

NO.31 SQUADRON, R.F.C. and R.A.F.

FROM 1915 to 1950

The formation of No.31 Squadron commenced in October 1915 when on the 11th inst. an Indian draft for the formation of "A" Flight and the nucleus of Aircraft Park was selected at Farnborough, Hants and sent on five days leave.

On November 16th the transport convoy left Farnborough for Birkenhead via Oxford and Castle Bromwich and on the 18th arrived at Birkenhead. The party embarked on "S.S. Elysia" and on December 2nd sailed disembarking at Bombay on the 26th. - The Officers on the strength of the Flight on arrival were:-

Capt. C.Y. McDonald	2nd Lt. O. Hughes
Capt. Colin Cooper	2nd Lt. Gordon-Dean
Lt. W. Eyre, Aircraft Park.	

The Flight was met at Bombay by Lieut. H. Tilley, 1st Batt. The Durham Light Infantry who had been selected for attachment with 2 N.C.O's and 8 men to instruct the personnel in Indian ways.

On January 3rd, 1916 the party entrained for Pir-Pai eleven miles west of Nowshera N.W.F. Province on the Nowshera-Peshawar Road and here the B.E.2C Flight went under canvas. Three machines "B.E.2C" were assembled and fitted with Bomb sights and racks, two of the machines also being fitted with Wireless sets.

On the 13th January, 1916 the General Officer Commanding the Division inspected the Squadron; this was the first inspection of any unit of The Royal Flying Corps in India.

Instructional Classes in URDU and PUSHTU were started for the men and quite a number took the examination at PESHAWAR in April with creditable results.

On January 20th Capt. McDonald made the first flight in "B.E.2C" No.445 and so commenced the History of Service flying in India. On the 21st, Capt. Colin Cooper and 2nd Lieut. Gordon-Dean took the air and on the 25th Lieut. Hughes made his first flight and reached a height of 7000 feet.

On February 5th the first two Army Officers (Capt. Skinner and Lt. Mayberry) arrived at the Squadron for a Course of Aerial Observation and during the following two years the Squadron was never without Officers under instruction.

On February 8th Capt. Colin Cooper, Lt. Hughes and Lt. Gordon-Dean looped the loop, the first time this had been done in India. The strength of the Squadron at the date was 6 Officers and 28 N.C.O's and men.

On February 23rd two machines, Capt. McDonald and Lt. Gordon-Dean flew to Peshawar to attend and demonstrate at a Durbar held by the CHIEF COMMISSIONER, North West Frontier Province - Sir George Rous Keppel at which all the Chiefs of the Trans-Border Tribes attended. It was most interesting to watch the faces of these Chiefs - hardy old Warriors - at first sight of the machines in flight. They said "the machines were only large birds and that no human being could possibly be inside them;" but when they witnessed the machines land and Sir George whom they knew so well, enter a machine, go for a flight and land safely again, their wonder and awe was indescribable; one very interesting remark they made was to the effect "that the day of the Robber and Murderer was at an end as the Raj, or Sirkar could get behind them and see all their doings.

On March 1st the Squadron had to abandon PIR-PIA owing to torrential rains which literally flooded the men out of their tents and a move was made to higher ground at RISALPUR, Stores and machinery being sent from SITAPUR to form the nucleus of Workshop and Repair Sections.

On March 7th Capt. Tilley was appointed Squadron recording Officer and A/Adjutant and on 31st March, 1917 appointed Acting Adjutant to the whole of the R.F.C. and on the 17th January, 1918 Wing Adjutant (52nd Wing) until May, when the Unit removed to SIMLA as a separate Unit under the Command of Lt. Colonel R. Campbell Heathcote.

On April 16th a scheme was laid out with C.R.A. PESHAWAR Division, for four weeks practice in co-operation between Aircraft and Artillery "M" Battery R.H.A. 24th Mountain Battery and 16 Bde. R.F.A. Only three weeks of this practice however were completed owing to a severe dust storm which wrecked most of the machines.

As this was a first trial of co-operation between Aeroplanes and Artillery in India difficulties were experienced owing to the ignorance on the part of the Observers of the different types of shell used, the rate of fire and the time of flight of the shell; and on the part of the gunners by their ignorance of the performance of an aeroplane. Lieut-Colonel L.A. Smith, R.F.A. definitely laid down in his report afterwards that:-

"A successful observer of Artillery fire could only be an Artillery Officer of some experience, who thoroughly knew what observations a Battery Commander required to fight his Battery effectively".

This first effort at Co-operation gave Headquarters enough work to carry on with for the next six months, compiling impossible instructions to be carried out by both arms. By the end of the year however, some sort of working procedure had been arranged for, to be experimented with at the next winter camp, to be held in December.

One material advantage however derived from the experience of this camp, was the series of inspired drawings relating to the more prominent mistakes, which are now hanging in the Officers Mess.

An extract from a casualty report dated 30/4/16 shows the state of the Squadron at that time.

"5 Machines on charge of "A" Flight of which of 2 are serviceable and 3 repairable.

5 Machines on charge of "B" Flight of which 1 is serviceable, 3 damaged and 1 totally wrecked."

The unrepairable machine being referred to as "Scrapped for Spares".

The General Staff now started to take a serious interest in the Squadron, and the following report was compiled for their benefit on the behaviour of the B.E.2C 90H.P. R.A.F.

(1) In the cold weather the machine proved fairly satisfactory. A considerably larger landing ground was found to be necessary than is required in England and France. Probably this is chiefly owing to the dryness of the atmosphere.

(2) In the hot weather it will be impossible to use these machines at all, except for two or three hours after dawn, and even then a very much larger landing ground is necessary than most of those now existing in the district.

For example on April 18th, at about 4.45 p.m. a machine with Pilot and Observer and a light wireless set ran 450 yards before leaving the ground, and then took approximately 15 minutes to climb the first thousand feet after which the climbing speed steadily improved.

The 90 h.p. R.A.F. engine has proved very liable to overheat in warm weather and in hot weather it will be quite impossible to run this engine at full power long enough to climb through the hot strata of air on the ground.

On June 17th "C" Flight consisting of five Officers and twenty-five British other Ranks arrived from England and were taken on the strength of the Squadron. "A" and "B" Flights had been formed out of the original Squadron which landed in 1915, with the addition of several Officers who had been posted since then, so that the Squadron was now practically up to its full strength in personnel.

Major C.R. Bradley now took over command and from the middle of June until the end of August the routine work of the Squadron consisted in the training of Observers, practice reconnaissances, wireless work, photography and gunnery.

It was now decided that RISALPUR should be a permanent Royal Flying Corps Station, and plans were got out and great preparations made for the building of permanent hangars, workshops and quarters. This scheme was put in hand straight away with the result that so much water was required in the erection of the buildings there was almost a drought in the Station.

In August Major Bradley made a tour of the North West Frontier Province with a view to arranging a series of emergency landing grounds. He visited all the country round KOHAT and BANNU, and later on toured through the KURRAM district to PARACHINNAR. He selected many of the landing grounds now in use on the frontier, including AKORA the scene of so many subsequent Artillery Practice Camps. He also selected the route and emergency landing grounds between JHELUM and RAWAL PINDI.

On September 19th the Squadron was inspected by General Salmond, the General Officer Commanding the Middle East Area. He was given a flight round the border in order to get an idea of the formation of the country in the North West Frontier Province.

During October and November the Kuki Khel Mohmands commenced to give trouble and threatened the KHYBER PASS. Aeroplanes were eagerly sought for by the General Staff for reconnaissance purposes and machines from 31 Squadron carried out continuous reconnaissances and bombing raids over HAFIZ KOR, THE GANDAB, and the ALIKANDI VALLEYS until to further facilitate operations, one flight was detached to SHABKADAR, where a temporary aerodrome had been constructed.

As this was the first "Show" which the Royal Flying Corps did in India, the complete summary of operations together with an actual copy of an observers report are given:-

Resumé of operations from 12th November to 18th November, 1916:-
13th inst., To-day four reconnaissances were carried out on the Mohmand frontier between ABAZAI and MICHNI to the depth of about six miles over the mountains: reports showed 200 enemy encamped about SHABAZ KHAM KOR, 900 about HAFIZ KOR, and 2000 finally reported on the Right and Left bank of SUBHAN KHWAR NULLAH at 9.30 a.m. with small parties of enemy between HAFIZ KOR and DAWAZAGAI.

14th inst., Further reconnaissances carried out throughout today showed considerable movement along the frontier hills, hangars were being built by the enemy in many places and on hill tops.

From JAIAL KOR to HAFIZ KOR, enemy had picketted every height with from 50 to 100 men on each, small parties moving about in the rear of this line.

North East of Point 1210, a party of over 1000 men apparently being addressed by a Mullah on a white horse; six columns, one of 400 men and the others of about 600 each seen approaching this assembly. Altogether enemy strength estimated during the day 5000 men.

A long reconnaissance was carried out up the GANDAB valley, as far as SHATI KHEL, some 20 miles over the mountains, showing unusual activity in the villages of GHALANI, SANGAR, KAWAJOSKOI and SHATI KHEL.

15th inst., Twelve machines co-operated on this day after flying out and landing on the SHABKADAR FORT ground, operations started by wireless machines reconnoitering for the enemy and then putting the guns on to them at once. About 10 a.m. the 74th Howitzer Battery engaged nine targets and O.K's were quickly found dispersing the enemy at once. After each burst of battery fire the enemy retired only to return later when the battery was engaged elsewhere, necessitating a return to the original target, and so on all day.

The 10th Brigade R.F.A. in a position west of SHABKADAR FORT working with a separate ground station engaged many targets in a similar manner with excellent effect.

In the afternoon three machines mounted with Lewis Guns engaged various targets and bodies of the enemy who were retiring, descending to about 200 feet, one pilot reports seven direct hits by his observer and a second observer accounted for four enemy.

At the same time four machines with bombs harrassed enemy parties and encampments further into the mountains. One encampment was hit and a convoy of camels and men was broken up; four of the camels were observed to fall into the Subhan Kwar Nullah.

Bombing was not effective against parties of men; machines returned to RISALPUR about 6 p.m.

16th inst., An early morning reconnaissance soon after dawn reported a great decease in the enemy numbers very few small parties were observed.

The 74th Battery were put on to small parties but no real targets were available. The battery only fired 14 rounds. At 4.30 p.m. three machines were ordered to bomb the village of MATUI KALI; nineteen bombs were released out of which fifteen were direct hits. The machines returned at 5.30 p.m.

17th inst., Two reconnaissances carried out during the morning from SHABKADAR, failed to find anything to report; the enemy had apparently split up and returned. Six machines were at SHABKADAR and an evening reconnaissance was sent out with the same result.

Machines returned to the aerodrome at RISALPUR at 5 p.m. 18th inst., Reconnaissances during the day failed to find any signs of the enemy.

In these actions the enemy were apparently armed with a fair percentage of good rifles, their fire was quite accurate and several machines were hit. One cylinder head was shot away and a petrol tank pierced but the fuel in the top tank enabled the pilot to reach SHABKADAR landing ground. An engine bearer was also pierced. The only casualty amongst machines during the week was the complete wreckage of one machine on its way back to RISALPUR when it came to ground with its engine apparently in perfect order, but the machine suddenly refused to hold the air; no defect in the rigging could be found owing to the wrecked condition of the machine. The pilot and passenger were unhurt.

During the whole of the year Officers were arriving from home, until by the end of the year the establishment was brought up to twenty-eight Officers and eighty-four other ranks.

The following are the Officers on the strength of the Squadron on December 31st, 1916.

Major	C.R.S.	Bradley.
Major	S.	Hutcheson.
Capt.	C.Y.	McDonald.
Capt.	D.R.	Hanlon.

Capt.	C.	Cooper.
Capt.	B.	Crossley.
Capt.	G.L.	Hunting.
Capt.	A.F.A.	Hooper.
Capt.	V.W.	Eyre.
Lieut.	P.G.H.	Fender.
Lieut.	H.A.	Tweedie.
Lieut.	H.E.	Fletcher
Lieut.	C.R.	Taylor.
Lieut.	V.P.	Cronyn.
Lieut.	L.C.	Boyd.
2/Lieut.	O.W.	Hughes.
2/Lieut.	W.A.	Harvey.
2/Lieut.	R.H.	Robinson.
2/Lieut.	F.G.M.	Williams.
2/Lieut.	L.J.	Mann (now Douglas-Mann, M.C.)
2/Lieut.	F.C.	Blunt.
2/Lieut.	A.J.C.	Spiers.
Lieut.	C.E.	Sherwin.
2/Lieut.	E.B.	Rice.
2/Lieut.	-	Robertson.
Lieut.	H.	Tilley.
Lieut.	O.S.	Waymouth.

Lieut. O.S. Waymouth, 121st Pioneers, who joined the Squadron on 1st October, 1916 for training as an Observer completed his training and qualified as an Observer on 1st January 1917, was employed as an Observer until 17th May, 1917 when he was appointed the first Squadron Equipment Officer and on the formation of the Wing he was appointed Wing Equipment Officer, May 1918.

WAZIRISTAN

As the Squadron operated over Waziristan on many occasions after 1916, it is thought that a brief description of that part of the North West Frontier would not be without interest.

Waziristan consists of a tract of Independent Territory lying between the North West Frontier Province and Afghanistan; in shape it is a rough parallelogram with an average length of 110 miles from North to South, and an average breadth of 60 miles.

In the North West and on the slopes of the two principal mountains, SHUIDAR and PIR GHAL, are thick forests and here and there grassy uplands which afford excellent grazing for the flocks and herds, which are the most valued possession of the tribesman. It is these which are the principal targets for machines operating over tribal country. The tribesman is an adept in the art of concealing himself and it is seldom that a good human target is found for bombs and machine guns. These flocks and herds, offer however an ideal target, and the strafing of these eventually persuades the bellicose tribesman to listen to reason, and to return to more peaceable pursuits than raiding, and the cutting up of picquets.

The remainder of the country is a maze of tangled mountains and ravines, which are all destitute of any vegetation.

There are six main valleys, which are reading from North to South as follows, The Kaiku, Tochi, Khaisora and Shaktu. These all run from West to East and are inhabited by Wazirs. Next comes the Tank Zam running from North to South where live most of the Mahsuds, and running into this valley is the Shahur which is divided between the Mahsuds and the Wana Wazirs. Lastly comes the Gomal which runs down from Baluchistan.

The inhabitants of Waziristan are all more or less of Afghan extraction, and are divided into two main divisions, these being the Mahsuds and the Wazirs. The former have always been our most formidable enemies on the Indian Frontier. They are a typical Highland race and in many respects they resemble the mediaeval Scots. The tribes are divided into clans and again into sections and sub-sections, every chief having his stronghold.

Although family feeling is strong, feuds between families are of short duration and where by any cause a family becomes destitute, the other families in the same section will invariably contribute towards restoring its prosperity.

Personal bravery is accounted the chief virtue, and compared with other tribes the Mahsuds are of a frank and open disposition, although they are past masters in the art of deceiving an enemy.

The vices of the Afridi are almost unknown and they are not fanatical, but are very impatient of any form of government. For this reason the only real control over them is exercised by leaders of successful raiding parties who uphold an example of great bravery. They are expert rifle shots and are almost now universally equipped with modern rifles, and plenty of ammunition. They make remarkably good shooting at aeroplanes in flight, swinging on to their target. On one occasion they produced two mountain guns which they used against the machines to the great amusement of the pilots and observers.

The country is a difficult one for aerial operations. Tribesmen on the ground can get excellent cover among the rocks and are almost invisible from above, while in many cases they can fire down on to machines from above.

The great heat and the height of the ground also present difficulties, and owing to the rocky and precipitous nature of the country forced landings are fraught with much danger. In addition forced landing and capture may result in mutilation and death by various unpleasant methods. With a view to minimising this risk officers are provided with Ransom or "Goli" chits, which promise a considerable sum for the return of the occupants of the machine to the nearest British post; always providing that they are in an intact condition.

1 9 1 7

The year 1917 opened with intensive Artillery Co-operation at Akora, in which all flights took part, the G.O.C. Northern Army being present, who reported very favourably on the proceedings.

Numerous wireless tests were carried out, messages being received up to 60 miles, and later on up to 80, 90 and eventually 100 miles.

On January 29th "A" Flight sent a detachment under Capt. Cooper, for duty in the Frontier stations in the Bannu and Derajat Brigade. A lashkar of 2000 Mahsuds had been reported as approaching Tank, from which place the flight carried out reconnaissances over Khirgai, Zam Post, Spiki, Gimi and Khuzma. This was to ensure that no hostile forces were approaching Tank from Jandola. Photographs were also taken of the frontier line forts.

The Political Agent of the district, reported that the arrival of the machines caused "stupendous" effect the beliefs commonly held among the frontier tribes being:-

(1) That aeroplanes did not exist at all.

(2) That if they did they were exclusively manned by Germans.

(3) That the preparations of forced landing grounds was a bluff.

(4) That no one but an expert could even sit in a machine.

These beliefs have now been dispelled and several thousand of the tribesmen have seen machines land and take off again with the Political Agent as a passenger whom they all know and recognise.

Comments from the tribesmen were to this effect:- The day of Judgment has arrived, - The Afghan Government is now nothing better than a pack of cards. - The day of robbers and outlaws is over.

On February 1st the Squadron was inspected by Lieut. General Sir G.M. Fitzpatrick, K.C.,S.I.,C.B., the Chief of the General Staff.

On February 5th the detached Flight moved to Dera Ismail Khan, and during the next few days carried out extensive reconnaissances over Tank, Draband, Drasyinda and Hatala.

On February 15th, one machine left for Lahore to carry out reconnaissances in the vicinity. It landed at Rawal Pindi on the way, at the request of the military authorities, where a demonstration was given to the inhabitants who had largely contributed to the Aeroplane Fund.

At 1.30 p.m. on Thursday, March 1st, the following message was received by telephone from the General Staff, 1st Peshawar Division:- "The Chief Commissioner requests that aeroplanes should be despatched to

Tank, in connection with reported approach of Mahsud lashkar to Sarwaki. Order Royal Flying Corps to dispatch two machines to Tank. They should be prepared to operate immediately under orders of G.O.C. Derajat Brigade".

The two machines left Rissalpur Aerodrome on the morning of the 2nd, and arrived safely at Tank at 10.30 a.m. that day having flown direct to Tank. Another machine joined them on the 6th. On the 15th they received orders from the G.O.C. Northern Army to return as the Mahsuds had dispersed.

On the 30th the Hon. G.B.A. Fell, the Military Adviser, paid an official visit, and was taken for a flight.

About this time experiments were carried out in communication of written messages to Aircraft, where no landing ground is available. This was done by means of a hook on the end of a wireless aerial of the machine. This was trailed over a wire stretched between two posts on the ground, with a message attached to the wire. The aerial was then wound in and the message detached by the observer.

This was found to give quite good results and a report was accordingly sent to the Director General of Ordnance in India at Simla.

About this time several changes took place in the Personnel of the Squadron. Captains C.Y. McDonald, V.W. Eyre, A.F. Hooper, D.R. Hanlon and Lieut. G.P.H. Fender, returned to Home Establishment, whilst Lieuts. L.G. Mann, W.A. Harvey and 2/Lieuts. R.M. Ranken and J.J. O'Farrell arrived from Egypt to join the Squadron.

On April 7th His Excellency, The Viceroy of India, Her Excellency, and all the Viceregal Staff, accompanied by Sir George Ross-Keppel, the Chief Commissioner of the North West Frontier Province, with his staff paid a visit to the Squadron, and inspected the Aircraft Park Workshops and Sheds and witnessed flying, whilst the Hon. Joan Thesiger, the Viceroy's daughter, was taken for a flight. The inspection lasted two hours and His Excellency was very interested and pleased with every thing he saw. An Album containing photographs of the visit was compiled by Lt. Blunt and the presentation was made by Major Bradley O/C 31st Squadron the actual handing over being made by Doreen Tilley, the little daughter of Capt. Tilley, the Adjutant to the Hon. Joan Thesiger who had been flown to Peshawar by Lt. Alec Tweedie for the presentation.

On April 10th trouble loomed up in the Mohmand country, and the Officer Commanding the Squadron flew over to Shabkadar to interview the G.O.C. with reference to operations.

Extracts from operations resumés round this date read:-

20th. One machine for reconnaissance over Mohmand Country.
    Two machines for wireless co-operation with Howitzer and
        Mountain batteries.
    The reconnaissance machine dispersed a body of 150 of the
        enemy with his Lewis Gun.

22nd. One machine under co-operation orders, ranged a Howitzer battery on Darwazagai village several O.K's obtained.

The Political Agent now received information that a Mullah, who was trying to collect men from the high country around, had failed in his object of trying to persuade them to come down and attack.

Further reconnaissances were carried out on the 22nd, 23rd and the 24th, but no enemy were seen and a wire was received from the G.O.C. Blockade Line to discontinue reconnaissances until further notice.

On April 25th Lieuts. Macklem and Legge Williamson reported their arrival from Egypt, and were posted to the Squadron to complete the establishment.

On May 4th orders were received from the G.O.C. Northern Army to despatch three machines to Tank, to operate against the Mahsuds who were reported to be collecting in British territory. Transport and personnel left the same afternoon and the machines, at dawn the following day arriving safely after a flight of 3 hours and 15 minutes.

On May 12th Major S. Hutchinson took over temporary command of the Squadron, from Major Bradley who was promoted Wing Commander and ordered home.

The three machines at Tank of "B" Flight carried out reconnaissances daily and on Saturday the 12th a blanket and tent encampment was observed close to the source of the Tor Manda Nola. The machine descended and fired 5 drums into a crowd of over a 1000 Mahsuds, who broke up and scattered, a good many of them being hit.

The following morning eight bombs were dropped on the same encampment, and four direct hits were observed. The next day the enemy had disappeared.

On the 15th a raiding party was reported across the Dera Ismail Khan to Tank Road, and machines had therefore to be taken into the Tank perimeter every evening, a distance of nearly a mile.

At 8 a.m. on the 15th, orders were received from G.O.C. Waziristan Field Force, to send three other machines to Tank to take part in the Military Operations on the 19th. The machines were despatched immediately but the operations had to be postponed on account of the river Gumal being in flood and not passable for troups.

On the 20th a convoy escorted by a column of Infantry and Guns crossed the Gumal river.

It appears that the whole object of the Military Operations which eventually took place, consisted of getting a convoy through to Kajuri Kach.

Five machines co-operated with the column escorting the convoy. A wireless station was sent on camels with the column, and communications were established. The heights on either side were searched, while the column was crossing the river.

On June 22nd "B" Flight was relieved by "C" before the pending opera-tions on June 5th.

On June 9th Capt. Fletcher, when flying solo near Haidari Kach, having dropped his bombs, observed 70 to 100 Mahsuds in the fields and hedges. His report states that this body was dispersed by flying low and firing his revolver at them.

The temperature at Tank had now reached 112 Degrees in the shade, and the hangars had to be roofed with grass mats.

Experiments were carried out with a view to using camels for the purpose of transporting R.A.F. hangars if necessary, and the following interesting report was received:-

"Difficulty was experienced with the triangles and the long poles, and the camel drivers asserted that these could not be carried on camels. A trial was therefore made, and on one occasion two poles were lashed one on each side of a camel. It was found that when the camel walked, a swaying motion was developed in the poles and the latter often came in contact with the camels head and neck. The rear end of the poles were then tied together so that the poles formed a "V" with the angle at the rear". This was found to be an improvement, but it was impossible to prevent altogether the swaying motion. On the second camel, two "D" were lashed together, their bases down-wards the rear being also lashed as in the case of the poles. The camel was found to be able to walk with very little discomfort. The conclusion arrived at was that the transport of hangars by camel would be possible if necessary, and that the total number of camels required to transport one hangar would be eighteen.

Maurice Farman machines had been experimented with during the last few months, and on the 11th June one was fitted with dual control with a view to using the machines for tuition purposes.

Operations against the Mahsuds were now further postponed. Sand Fly Fever and Sunstroke had raised the percentage of sick, and it was necessary to meet this setback, by increasing the personnel out at Tank.

Meantime constant reconnaissances were being carried out over the enemy territory, and communications were kept with the advancing columns, and with the Headquarters of the Waziristan Field Force at Jandola.

Dust here at times completely obscured the hills on either side, but did not interfere with the vertical observation of the Nullahs, while on some mornings on account of the heat, machines took as much as 45 minutes to climb 4000 feet.

The whole of the area had been photographed by the Flight at Tank from which a map was made, and delivered by air to the G.O.C. of the Waziristan Field Force at Jandola, where the new aerodrome had now been completed.

On June 24th a column moving from Shrawani towards Kharsan met with serious opposition. Lieut. Boyd reconnoitering high ground dropped bombs successfully on the villages in advance of the column, and fired into a party of men near Darsheli, causing about 100 casualties.

Lieut. Robinson with Captain Kitson, as observer discovered about a hundred Mahsuds holding a ridge, in a very strong position. Coming down to 100 feet, he flew three times up and down the ridge, using his machine gun causing many casualties and forcing the enemy to retire and thereby allowing our troops to advance. Many other small bodies of the enemy were scattered later by machine gun fire. Lieut. Robinson's machine was hit five times by rifle bullets. The enemy's shooting was apparently very erratic.

On the 25th Capt. Fletcher, who was up solo with bombs and a Lewis Gun lashed to the side near the pilot's seat, successfully bombed two villages and scattered a small party of the enemy, followed up our column returning to Barwand.

On the 26th Capt. Fletcher with Lieuts. Robinson, Boyd and Rankin, bombed Makin and Marobi getting direct hits and doing considerable damage. All four machines returned safely. Makin is the second largest village in the Mahsud territory, and is built in terraces on the hill-side, at an elevation of about 6400 feet, From Tank to Makin is about 46 miles in a direct line. There is practically no ground upon which a machine could make a forced landing safely from Jandola to Makin, a distance of 28 miles, the whole country being mountainous and intersected with steep ravines. Cultivation around villages is very scarce and consists of fields built in small terraces, situated along the banks of a stream or cut out of the hill side.

On the 27th a wire was received from the G.O.C. Waziristan Field Force, to cease bombing raids or any further aerial activity until further orders.

A wire received some hours later reads:- "The G.O.C. Waziristan Field Force congratulates the R.F.C. on the successful raids in Mahsuds territory. These raids have had a great effect, and this morning a messenger arrived from Kangrim, asking that they might be stopped, while peace terms were being considered. He says that one bomb killed twelve men, wounded another and destroyed some cattle. If the Mahsuds come to terms a full share of the credit will be due to the Royal Flying Corps".

Meanwhile, in the remainder of the Squadron, at Risalpur, training was being carried out as usual, but in concentrated form. Photography, tests flights, Artillery practice with puffs for N.C.O. Observers, Long Distance reconnaissances, and formation flights, were carried out daily, in order to keep the flights well up to the mark in case they were called upon to relieve the Flight at Tank.

On July 14th it was officially announced that the Mahsuds were handing over their arms, and that satisfactory terms had been arranged and that peace had been declared. Political Agents stated that the Mahsuds were disgusted with their Mullahs, who told them that the British were a waning power, instead of which enormous numbers of troops had entered their country and had terrified them by dropping bombs from the sky on them and their village

On July 19th preparations were commenced for the evacuation of the troops, although the machines were still warned to stand by in case of treachery.

Lieut. Robinson flew Capt. Wauchope Royal Engineers over Jandola, Hadri Kach, and Nill Kach in order to find a new route.

Capt. Fletcher, solo at the request of the General Staff, flew over with a dozen tins of condensed milk, and some medicine to Nill Kach, for the use of the sick, who were in great need of supplies. Capt. Fletcher landed safely on not too good ground and returned after having delivered the supplies asked for.

Major S. Hutcheson left for Tank on the 21st to inspect the detachments and to make arrangements for future requirements if any.

On July 28th in answer to a wire from the G.O.C. Waziristan Field Force asking for recommendations for mentions in despatches, the following reply was sent. "Capt. Fletcher whose example on the ground and in the air under unknown and trying conditions, has been largely responsible for the success of the operations carried out by the flight under his command. Lieut. Robinson, for flying down Nullas and clearing ridges with Lewis Gun and for successful bombing flights on several occasions over difficult country. Capt. Kitson, observer, for good Lewis Gun work on the 24th against the enemy. Sergt. Newfor the able and cheerful way he carried out his duties, in keeping machines serviceable under trying conditions. Air Mechanics Haynes and Maltby for general good work under trying conditions".

On July 29th Lieut. Rice on a B.E.2C, proceeded to Parachinnar picking up fuel at Kohat, in order to test the landing ground there, which is 5800 feet above the sea level. Landing quite safely, the height above sea level made apparently no difference.

On July 30th an altitude test was carried out with an F.E.2B, the result being 7500 feet in 45 minutes, this test was made under hot weather conditions in the middle of the day. The machine behaved better than a B.E.2C in the bumps caused by the hot air. On the following day another test was carried out with the same machine, resulting in an increase of 1000 feet in the 45 minutes, this being due to climbing the machine at a steeper angle.

The situation on the Mohmand border and also in the Mahsud territory was now comparatively quiet, and a message was received from the G.O.C. Waziristan Field Force to the following effect:- "On account of the wonderful moral effect and usefulness of aeroplanes on this Frontier, the G.O.C. Waziristan Field Force has asked for details required for buildings necessary to house one Flight at Tank, so that bombing raids etc., can be carried out by the Squadron from Risalpur if required in the future, in order that the flight on arrival, may find suitable accommodation at Tank".

A landing ground was prepared at Mansal in one, in order that machines could fly over and keep in touch with the G.O.C. every day.

On the 11th August, a special Order of the Day was issued by the Commander-in-Chief which included the following remarks about the Royal Flying Corps:-

"For the first time, the tribesmen on this Frontier, have felt the power of the Royal Flying Corps, which carried out its duties with the dash and daring, to which the Army has been accustomed".

On the 5th August Lieut. Sare Soar reported his arrival to the Squadron and took over the photographic section.

On August 10th Lieut. Bennet reported from England and was posted to the Stores section.

On August 14th Lieut. Robinson went to the School of Mountain Welfare at Abbotabad to lecture on the work of the R.F.C. and the various methods of the Co-operation.

Everyone is familiar with the stilted form in which Stores etc., are marked, but on the 26th September a letter came through from Dera Ismail Khan, which shows that there is nothing which cannot be classified by the machines like Quartermaster. The letter reads as follows:-

"Please remit to this office the sum of Rupees Forty-nine on account of the value of One Coffin Large supplied for the late Sergt. C------------. An early settlement is required."

The remainder of the year from September onwards was taken up with training in Wireless, Photography, Reconnaissance, Pigeons, Formation Stunting, Gunnery, Cross Country Flying etc. Many expeditions were also made in search of Landing Grounds round the Frontier.

On December 6th Lieut. Robinson and 2nd A.M. Cameron were flying over the Aerodrome. The machine had just completed one loop and was entering another, when the Starboard Main Planes were seen to fold back along the fuselage. The machine came down in a spin and on crashing to earth burst into flames. The pilot and mechanic were killed instantly.

At the end of the year, the Squadron had a strength of 64 machines of which 26 were B.E.2C's, 34 Henri Farmans, 3B.E.2E's and 1 F.E.2B. The total engine strength was 79.

The following officers were shown on the strength of the Squadron during 1917.

Major	N.M. Martin.	2/Lieut.	Watkins.
Major	S. Hutcheson.	2/Lieut.	Hillman.
Major	R.G.H. Murray, M.C.	2/Lieut.	Oddie.
Capt.	Fletcher.	2/Lieut.	Green.
Capt.	Colin Cooper.	2/Lieut.	Jamieson.
Capt.	Bomerjee.	2/Lieut.	Kirk.
Capt.	W.B. Crossley.	2/Lieut.	King.
Capt.	Kitson.	2/Lieut.	Searle.

Lieut. G.H. Shortridge.
Lieut. E.H. Grant.
Lieut. O'Farrell.
Capt. W.W. Tullis.
Lieut. Sare Soar.
Lieut. Thompson.
Lieut. Guilbert.
Lieut. Welch.
Lieut. Gompertz.
Lieut. E.B. Rice.
Lieut. A.J.O. Spiers.
Lieut. Cambridge.
Lieut. F.G.M. Williams.
Lieut. F.R. Cook.
Lieut. K.H. Brown.
Lieut. G.M. Eastley.
Lieut. G.R. Travis.
Lieut. Parkinson.

2/Lieut. Cumming.
2/Lieut. Keeping.
Capt. H. Tilley (Adjt.)
Lieut. O.S. Waymouth (E.O.)

The following officers left for Aden on November 3rd.

Capt. G. Sherwin, M.C.
Lieut. C.H. Tayler.
Lieut. L.J. Mann.
Lieut. Thomas.
Lieut. Owden.

The first landing by Air in Amritsar was successfully accomplished by Lt. Thomas and Lt. Kirk, flying B.E.2E's - An emergency landing ground being marked out on the polo ground, various notabilities were taken for short Flights and a Civic welcome was accorded the two Officers.

1918

The year 1918 was comparatively uneventful, except for operations in the neighbourhood of Dera Ghazi Khan.

During January much work was done inspecting and photographing all the aerodromes and forced landing grounds on the Frontier. Work on new landing grounds was also commenced and made considerable progress. The hills on the neighbouring portion of the Frontier were reconnoitred closely, and much time was spent in practice formation flying and bomb dropping. Some experimental work was also carried out with the Klaxon Horn, with encouraging results.

On February 19th the Squadron supplied a detachment to co-operate with the 2nd Divisional Artillery at Rawal Pindi, Wireless was used, and each day eight shoots were carried out, four being pre-arranged and four impromptu. The position of the ground targets was signalled by wireless, giving the pin-point, by smoke ball, by Verey's light, and by the "H" method. The camp was an entire success.

On February 25th a practice camp was commenced at Akora with the 1st (Peshawar) Divisional Artillery. This camp only lasted five days. On three of these days the targets and corrections were signalled by map squares and wireless, and on the other two days they were signalled by Verey's light and Klaxon Horn. On the 26th, an observer successfully ranged two batteries simultaneously with the Klaxon Horn. This system has obvious advantages in a moving battle and worked quite successfully except in the case of a strong reverse wind. Corrections were sent from 3000 feet under favourable weather conditions.

On March 18th the C.O. carried out a climbing test with the B.E.2E. The machine reached 6000 feet in $10\frac{1}{2}$ minutes in 10,000 feet in 32 minutes, finally reaching 12,800 feet.

On March 5th a telegraphic request was received from the Northern Command, for two aeroplanes to proceed to Dera Ghazi Khan. This part of the country was practically unknown as far as the R.F.C. was concerned, and Capt. O. Hughes at once left for Lahore by air and from thence went by rail to Multan and by tender to Ghazi Khan as a base and despatched a wire for the two machines to arrive on the 11th. Meantime stores, spare parts and personnel were despatched by rail to Ghazi Ghat, arriving on the 8th. The two machines landed on the 11th, and on the 12th, a machine carried out a reconnaissance of the Fort Munro Passes, and also dropped a message for our troops at Sakki Sawar.

On the 13th, Rakhni Village and a party of the enemy near Bawatta Post were bombed by two machines. On the 15th and 16th, Naharkot and Vitakri were bombed, on the latter day with great effect. On the 15th information was received that the enemy was attacking Fort Munro and both machines again left the ground, but thick clouds and rain on the mountains prevented them from getting any information. Much trouble was experienced owing to the boggy nature of the ground, and the smallness of the aerodromes. On the 24th, a machine was completely crashed owing to engine failure and the small size of the aerodrome.

On the 25th, orders were received to bomb a hostile gathering near Barkham, Capt. Hughes carried this out and bombs were observed to fall among a crowd of 100 people. On the 26th a reconnaissance along the Wanga Range observed an encampment of 25 tents and also 50 men. On the 28th, another machine piloted by Lieut. Legge-Wilkinson, arrived by air from Risalpur, to take the place of the machine previously crashed. Other successful reconnaissances were carried out on March 26th and 31st and on April 1st and 2nd.

On April 3rd, one machine bombed Kahan, the capital of the Murrie district. No further co-operation was required. On April 17th, the machines returned to Risalpur by air, the ground party following and arriving at Risalpur by rail on the 24th. The following officers took part in these operations, Capt. O. Hughes., Lieut. Brown and Lieut. Legge-Wilkinson.

On April 6th the Commander in Chief inspected the Squadron at Risalpur.

On June 14th, the following extract appeared in the London Gazette, "The following name is mentioned in a dispatch from General Sir S.H.H. Allenby, dated April 3rd, 1918. Capt. D.F. Massey!"

On Sept 6th the following reports on the Squadron at it's annual inspection were published.

Inspecting Officer and Divisional Commanders Report. Physical appearance satisfactory. The men are well turned out and are well disciplined. Musketry has just been carried out. Interior economy and internal condition of the Squadron are in all respects satisfactory. The Squadron is ably commanded and well officered. The personnel is keen and efficient. The Squadron is always proving its ability, and a very good tone exists, as should be the case in the Royal Corps.

Remarks by the General Officer Commanding Northern Command. Very useful work was done with the Waziristan Field Force, and later with the Murri Expedition. Good progress has been made in practising artillery co-operation and infantry co-operation at the practice camps and during Brigade training. The Squadron is in a creditable state of efficiency and is always ready to adopt and study new methods.

On the 27th of September, the following extract appeared in the London Gazette.

"H.M. the King has been graciously pleased to confer the undermentioned rewards for gallantry and distinguished service.

Awarded the Distinguished Flying Cross.

Capt. Hubert Ernest Fletcher.

Lieut. Edward Robinson. (since deceased)."

On October the 5th, a musical and dramatic society was formed in the Squadron, but no trace can be found of its activities. Perhaps its spirit still lives today in the famous Squadron Jazz Band which delights the followers of Terpischore in Peshawar.

On November 18th, the following Special Routine Order was published by Capt. O. Hughes, commanding the Squadron "Special Routine Order No.17 dated 13/11/18 by the Director of Aeronautics in India is republished for communication to all ranks.

The following message has been received by Lord Weir from His Majesty the King. "In this supreme hour of Victory I send greetings and heartfelt congratulations to all ranks of the Royal Air Force. Our Aircraft have been ever in the forefront of battle. Pilots and Observers have consistently maintained the offensive throughout the ever changing fortunes of the day, and in the War Zones our gallant dead have lain always beyond the enemies lines or far out to sea. Our far flung Squadrons have flown over Home Waters and Foreign Seas, the Western and Italian Battle lines, the Mountains of Macedonia and Gallipoli and Palestine, Rhineland and the plains of Mesopotamia. The forests and swamps of East Africa, the North West Frontier of India and the Deserts of Arabia, Sinai and Daruf. The birth of the Royal Air Force with it's wonderful expansion and development will ever remain - one of the most remarkable developments of the Great War. Everywhere by God's help, officers men, and women of the Royal Air Force have splendidly maintained our just cause and the value of their assistance to the Navy, the Army, and the Home Defences has been incalculable. For all their magnificent work, self sacrifice, and devotion to duty, I ask you on behalf of the Empire to thank them".

The following reply has been sent to the Air Ministry. "Your telegram dated 12th, instant conveying His Majesty's gracious message received. All ranks R.A.F. in India profoundly stirred, their devotion to His Majesty remains ever imperishable."

From November 22nd until December 1st, a holiday was granted by the Commander in Chief, on the occasion of the Armistice.

On December 1st, Major E.L. Millar took over command of the Squadron from Capt. O. Hughes.

The following officers were on the strength of the Squadron at the end of 1918.

Major   E.L. Millar.
Capt.   C. Hughes.
Capt.   R.H. Shears.
Capt.   G.R. Travis.
Lieut. L.C. Boyd.
Lieut. E.H. King.
Lieut. C.N. Thompson.
Lieut. F.N. Whiteley.
Lieut. E.H.P. Jolly.
Lieut. R.M. Rankin.
Lieut. V.H. Toulmin.
Lieut. A.V.H. Gompertz.
Capt.   E.M. Ashton.
Lieut. S.J. Bellamy.
Lieut. G.S. Barker.
2/Lt.   E.T. Crosslet.
2/Lt.   C.D. Longfellow.
2/Lt.   J.L. Kirby.
2/Lt.   W.W.E. Neville.
2/Lt.   D.W. Long.
2/Lt.   L.C. Dodkins.
2/Lt.   H.D. Scowcroft.
Lieut. H.B.H. Dickinson.
2/Lt.   D.J.C. Hutton.
2/Lt.   L.G. Hoare.
2/Lt.   R. Hayward.
Lieut. D.F. Histon.
2/Lt.   J. Platt.

2/Lt. W.F. Stewart.
2/Lt. N. Burke.
2/Lt. S. Moyles.
2/Lt. G.A. Body.
2/Lt. D. Thompson.
2/Lt. R.A. Williams.

---

1 9 1 9

At the beginning of 1919 the Squadron was commanded by Major
E.L. Miller, M.B.E. and was equipped with B.E.2E. and B.E.2C. machines
and one A.W. with 160 Beardmore engine.

In January "A" Flight sent a detachment of four machines to Tank,
where they carried out Artillery co-operation practices with mountain
batteries, contact patrol practice with the infantry, and some reconnaissance
flights. They returned to Risalpur about the middle of February.

In February 1919 Lieut. Colonel R. Campbell Heathcote the Wing
Commander whilst selecting landing grounds in Central India was mauled by
a Tiger whilst he was out shooting near Jubbulpore, he had wounded the Tiger
and whilst following it up the Tiger jumped on him, he was saved by another
officer of the party shooting the Tiger dead, but Lieut. Colonel Campbell
was badly mauled and was invalided to England.

In February and March the Squadron was engaged in carrying out a
considerable amount of Artillery co-operation practices with Mountain
batteries at Hutti and Akora.

Some tests seem to have been carried out with propellors, and an
extract reads "Airscrew test. Maximum Revs. in air 1625 at 56 M.P.H. Climb
to 11000 ft in 49 minutes".

Brigadier General M.D.K. MacEwen, C.M.G.,D.S.O., commanding the
Royal Air Force in India, inspected the Squadron on March 2nd, and left by
air for Lahore on the following day. In March three machines were sent to
Rawal Pindi for Artillery co-operation practices. The pilots were Lieuts.
Thompson, Bellamy and Barker.

Two machines went to Delhi on March 20th, for escort duty during the
visit of Admiral Lord Jellicoe the pilots being Lieuts. Junor and Kirby.
Another machine was flown at Delhi by Major Millar.

Up to April 5th, the Squadron continued the usual programme of
training in Flying and Co-operation.

The remainder of the year was a busy time for the Squadron as events
of importance followed one another in quick succession. The first event of

the series of riots at Amritsar, full details of which are unobtainable as they were never made public. Even the official resumé is very brief and leaves a lot to imagination.

On April 10th, two machines piloted by Lieuts. Thompson and Vincent left Risalpur for Lahore and landed there at 15.30 hours. At 17.00 hours a reconnaissance was made of Amritsar and it was reported that the station and several buildings had been burnt down. At 19.00 hours a large body of Indians assembled in Lahore City and marched into the English Quarter. Although fired on by troops they did not disperse and a night reconnaissance was carried out by Lieut. Col. Minchin. Owing to the machine not being fitted with parachute flares, the information gathered was purely negative, the approaches to the English Quarter were, however, reported clear.

As the situation in the Lahore district appeared to be getting serious, one Flight was dispatched from Risalpur, and arrived on the afternoon of the 11th. The pilots were Lieuts. Murgatroyd, Longfellow, Junor, Kirby, Allen and Dodkins, with 2/Lieut. Platt as observer.

A reconnaissance at dawn on the 11th, showed that there were two large crowds, one in the Bazaar and one round the Golden Temple. Other reconnaissances throughout the day reported that these crowds were slowly dispersing. The General Staff could not communicate with Amritsar and asked for two machines to be placed at their disposal for taking orders to the G.O.C. Troops there. Lieuts. Oddie and Thompson performed these duties and returned with despatches to Lahore.

On March 12th, the inhabitants were still rioting and it was decided to send a strong column into the city to seize various strong points and hold them. The column was to be supported by a low flying patrol of four machines with 20 lb. Hale bombs and machine guns, with the understanding that if a red Verey Light was fired by the Officer Commanding the column, bombs were to be dropped in the direction in which the light was fired. This patrol was up for $2\frac{1}{2}$ hours, but was not called upon to co-operate. Other reconnaissances were carried out over Amritsar, Kasur and Lahore. Lieut. Junor left for Delhi, where he reported to the District Commissioner, whilst Lieuts. Kirby and Longfellow flew to Ferozepore and reported to the Officer Commanding troops at that station. Despatches were carried by Lieut. Wells to Amritsar and an answer brought back the same day.

On the 13th reconnaissances were carried out and the situation was found to be comparatively quiet; the machines at Ferozepore and Amritsar returned to Lahore.

On the morning of the 14th, Lieuts. Thompson, Longfellow and Wells flew back to Risalpur. Later the same morning fresh disturbances were reported at Gujranwalla and three machines were sent out to disperse the crowd and aid the civil authorities. Capt. Carberry with Lieuts. Oddie and Vincent left Lahore at 14.00 hours with bombs and machine guns. On arrival at their destination the station and several buildings were found to be in flames, but as the crowd was dispersing only the first machine dropped its bombs. All three machines then combined to fire on small bodies of Indians who were in the open and were going back to the surrounding villages.   Capt. Carberry's report reads as follows:-

15.10   Gujranwalla...Railway Station on fire, bales of goods burning.
        Passenger train on up line in station appeared to be on fire.
        English Church and four houses on the East of Railway burning.
        All these are still burning at 15.50 hours.

15.20   Village N.W. of Gujranwalla...Dropped three bombs on a party of Indians
        150 strong outside village 2 miles N.W. of Gujranwalla. One bomb
        failed to explode. The others fell near party, which scattered.
        3 casualties seen and 50 rounds machine gun fired into village.

15.30   Village 1 mile S. of above. Party of 50 Indians outside village.
        2 bombs dropped. One only exploded within 10 yards of the party.
        No casualties seen. 25 rounds of machine gun fired into village.
        Party disappeared into the village. About 200 Indians in fields near
        a large red building on N.W. outskirts of the town. One bomb dropped
        which burst in courtyard of house. Several people appeared to be
        wounded. 30 rounds of machine gun fired into party which took cover
        in the house.

15.40   Gujranwalla...2 bombs which failed to explode dropped on large crowd
        of Indians in S. of town. 100 rounds of machine gun fired into parties
        of Indians in the streets. At 5.50 when machines left for Lahore no
        Indians could be seen in the streets. Station occupied by police.
        Landed aerodrome.

16.45   Lahore...Information has since been received that 12 men were killed
        by bombs in and around Gujranwalla.

                        (Signed) F.F. Minchin, Lieut. Col. Commanding 52nd
                                              Wing. Royal Air Force.

                        (Signed) D.H.M. Carberry, Captain Observer.

On the 15th reconnaissances were carried out, and on subsequent days until
the beginning of May. There was nothing to report and the machines then
returned to Risalpur.

    No sooner were these riots concluded than rumours were heard of an
impending Afghan war, and on May 3rd information was received from the N.W.
Frontier that the Afghans were about to declare a Jehad, being inspired by
false reports as to the internal conditions in India.

    On the 4th the Squadron received orders to keep two machines in
readiness to take part in the suppression of any aggressive movement on the
part of the Afghan troops assembling on the frontier.

    Hostilities were formally declared on May 6th, and Lieut. Col. Minchin,
commanding 52nd Wing immediately proceeded to Peshawar to confer with the
commander of the North West Frontier Force on points of co-operation.

    Major Millar was attached to Frontier Force H.Q. as Liaison Officer.

An extract from the resumé of operations reads:-

"The employment of aeroplanes, which were of the B.E. type at the commencement of operations was in a measure limited by the mountainous nature of the country over which the force was operating: but reconnaissance bombing, machine gunfire and photography were constantly carried on. Machines received a hot reception in the early period of our co-operation, due partly to the intrepidity of the pilots and partly to the good markmanship of the Afridi tribes who are far superior to the Afghans in sniping and sharpshooting. The height of the hills over which the machines were working also brought the latter into easy reach for close shooting.

On May 6th a reconnaissance was asked for over the Afghan side of the border, and three machines were employed. The enemies distributions were located and reported on. Machines received a very hot reception and came back with many bullet holes. The enemy were located in the heights of the range bordering the Khyber Pass and were apparently based on Loe Dakka.

On the 7th and 8th no work was asked for but on the 9th, a most striking and effective bombing raid was carried out on the enemies base at Dacca. All available machines, sixteen in number, made as many visits as they could possibly accomplish and the enemy was remorselessly harassed from morning until late in the evening. The casualties reported by agents reached some 600 men and the destruction of two elephants constitutes a unique record in the annals of aeroplane bombing history. It was later ascertained that the Afghan Commander-in-Chief's brother, a Mullah and a Malik were among the killed. On this day no less than a ton and a quarter of bombs were dropped, 1151 rounds of ammunition were fired into the enemy and 14 plates were exposed. The total days flying reached 60 hours 10 minutes. Three machines were brought down on our side of the lines. Of these Capt. Carberry on the A.W. forced landed and crashed, and Lieut. Keeping got a bullet in the sump of his engine which caused a forced landing.

Up to the 16th bombing and reconnaissance with ground strafing were carried out daily. On May 13th a Handley Page was sent from Lahore to participate in the offensive. Unfortunately before it could be used it was caught in a storm and destroyed in spite of all efforts to save it. Lorries were placed between it and the probable direction of the storm, and it was carefully picketted down, but the violence of the storm assumed such proportions that the strain of the screw pickets broke one wing and before it could be seized and possibly held down, it was thrown on its back and lay at the mercy of the storm. The gale was of sufficient strength to break several windows in Risalpur and it was the greatest misfortune possible that the storm should have arisen on the night of the machine's arrival.

On the 17th all available machines that could manage the distance from Risalpur to Jellabad were employed in creating an effect with bombs while the machines over which there was doubt were employed on nearer objectives.

On this raid the machines escorted each other in pairs in case of trouble. One of the pairs, Lieuts. Oddie and Villiers had an experience which fortunately ended in comedy. The latter was an ex R.A.F. officer who

had volunteered his services for the Afghan War. Both these officers forced
landed. Lieut. Villiers seeing some Indian troops thought that they were
hostile and walked towards them, revolver in one hand and ransome chit in the
other, when a voice from behind a boulder said in broad Somerset "I hope you
ain't 'urt Zur".

Lieut. Oddie landed at Dacca which was now in our hands and flew the
machine away later.

During the period from May 4th to May 17th, no less than 264 hours
55 minutes was done. The total weight of bombs dropped was 5868 lbs., 62
photographs were taken and 4475 rounds of machine gun ammunition were fired.
The weather was comparatively mild for the time of the year, and atmospheric
conditions over the Khyber were very severe, and even turned two machines
completely upside down in flight. The next event of importance was an
extensive bombing raid on Jallalabad on May 20th. The Amirs Palace was hit
and several bombs were dropped in the grounds adjoining. Four direct hits
were obtained on troops in close formation. These broke ranks on the approach
of the machines but not in time to escape the effect of the bombs. A very
large number of casualties resulted. About 150 bombs were dropped on military
billets in the town whence much firing had been directed on our machines.
A deputation of Afridis and Mohmands who had arrived to discuss their co-
operation and to receive arms and ammunition were left in possession of the
town, and made the most of their opportunity by thoroughly looting the bazaar.

Information was received later which indicated the almost complete
demoralisation of the Afghan troops and tribesmen as a result of offensive
action by aircraft. Jallalabad was deserted by its population and garrison,
as a result of this raid and messages describing the destruction of Jallalabad
were reported to have had a great deal to do with the inducing of large enemy
forces to retire from the Dacca front without taking any offensive.

On May 4th Capt. Halley with a crew consisting of one observer and
three mechanics made a very successful flight to Kabul in the V.1500 Handley-
Page which flew from England to India. The flight commenced at 3.39 a.m.
and Kabul was reached at 6.30 a.m. The Amirs Palace was bombed successfully
and the machine landed at Risalpur at 8.50 a.m. Reconnaissances and bomb
raids were carried on from Risalpur until the cessation of hostilities early
in June. An Armistice was then made and Peace was signed on August the 8th.

Atmospheric conditions were a source of interference to our aeroplanes
over the hilly country of the Frontier. With the advent of the hot weather
these adverse conditions increased to such an extent that flying was almost
impossible at the end of May, it being almost impossible to leave the ground
after 9.30 a.m. Dust storms were also a source of considerable trouble.
The temperature in May reached 114 degrees in the shade. As an instance in
June, Lieut. Vincent was flying over the Kohat Pass at about 10 o'clock in
the morning, in an 80 h.p. Le Rhone Avro. Owing to air disturbances the
machine, giving full power, sank to the road which runs at about two thousand
feet above sea level, and Lieut. Vincent had to fly along the winding road
for about half a mile, bouncing his wheels at intervals, until eventually the
machine climbed a little, and he was eventually able to reach Risalpur safely.
He did not land as the pass was closed and the inhabitants extremely hostile.

By the good offices of the Chief Commissioner, N.W.F.P., and his Agent Sir Abdul-Q-ayaum, the two missing officers, Lieuts. Barker and Hoare, who were forced to land in Bazar Valley, on the 14th of May, whilst carrying out a reconnaissance, were brought back from captivity in the Afridi country, after many trying experiences. Their ransom cost the Indian Government 30,000 Rupees.

On May 26th a fresh development occurred involving most of the Southern Tribes of the Buffer states, and necessitating the active employment of aircraft. Nadir Khan, in the early stages of his rapid moves had enlisted the sympathy of most of the tribes. The situation therefore was threatening and machines were dispatched from Risalpur to Kohat although at the time it was very difficult to spare them. The energy with which the pilots set about their task effectively deprived the Afghan General of the support of the tribes who lived in dread of aeroplanes, and he was eventually driven off. Three machines, piloted by Lieuts. Vincent, Keeping and Harris left Risalpur for Kohat on the 26th, and these were followed on the 28th by six more, piloted by Lieuts. Junor, Murgatroyd, Dodkins, Kirby and Pipe, with Lieuts. Curry and Cox as observers. Lieut. Vincent's machine was so badly shot about on his first reconnaissance that he had to return to Risalpur on the 27th. At this time Thal was in a state of siege and Parachinar was cut off completely from all communication.

A Brigade of Infantry and R.F.A. were marching to the relief of Thal.

From the date of arrival at Kohat until the 31st intensive bombing and machine gunning was carried out in the neighbourhood of Thal, with a view to shaking the morale of the enemy, and messages were dropped on Thal stating that relief would not be long delayed. On June 1st four machines successfully co-operated with the Thal relieving Column, bombing and machine gunning objectives out of the range of the Infantry, and giving targets to the Artillery. By 10 a.m. Thal was relieved. The pilots of these machines were Lieuts. Kirby, Murgatroyd, Dodkins and Curry.

All the machines landed on Thal aerodrome in the course of the morning, Lieut. Kirby was the first to arrive at 8.45 a.m. having had an interesting race with an armoured car to be first into Thal. This he won by two minutes, but was forced to take off again as, almost immediately he came under the fire of hostile guns and rifles. The co-operation of these machines during the relief was so successful that it was accomplished with almost negligible casualties to the column.

On the 28th Lieut. Keeping with Lieut. Cox as observer, landed at Miramshah, during a reconnaissance, to refill with petrol, and crashed taking off. In consequence there was said to be a Mullah at Miramshah who could cast spells over aircraft. A machine was accordingly sent on the 2nd June, to bomb targets in the vicinity and lower the prestige of the Mullah. The pilot was Lieut. Curry and such was the moral effect of this that villagers who had been hostile suddenly brought in gifts of sheep, milk, eggs and fowls.

The following is a copy of a letter received on June 3rd, by the Officer Commanding R.A.F. Detachment at Kohat from the G.O.C., 45th Infantry

Brigade, and commanding Field Force at Thal.

"Just a line to thank you for your splendid co-operation in helping me to relieve Thal. But for your excellent information and your accurate shooting and bombing, my task would have been infinitely harder. Please convey my gratitude to all under your command".

Reconnaissance was carried out daily until June 15th when the detachment was withdrawn to Risalpur.

A situation almost identical with that of Thal arose in the beginning of June, the place being Jandola in the Darajat area, the enemy consisting chiefly of Mahsuds, Jandola being in a state of seige. This necessitated a flight being sent to Tank in order to co-operate with the Waziristan Force, in its relief of the beleaguered garrison. About the 5th and 6th, four machines proceeded to Tank, the pilots being Captain Butler, Lieuts. Vincent, Wells and Longfellow. Other machines joined them but left for Bannu almost at once. The only officers who actually took part in the operations from Tank were Capt. Butler and Lieuts. Vincent and Curry.

The transport of this detachment had a long and trying journey to accomplish before it reached Tank on June 6th, and a great deal of heat-stroke and prostration was experienced. The maximum average temperature during this detachment was 123 degrees in the shade and no ice was available. Owing to lack of spares the machines were frequently flown without tyres and many landings were made on the rims.

On the 7th reconnaissances were attempted towards Jandola, but Lieut. Vincent was the only pilot who succeeded on account of heavy mists. He was signalled to by helio and flag but only succeeded in reading the word "water". It was evident from this that they had run short of water. He reported this to General Milne, O.C. Tank Column who instructed him to drop a message to the effect that on the following day he would bomb and fire upon the enemy, and that they were to make an effort to obtain water from a stream about 200 yards from the fort, while this was being done. This was successfully carried out on the 7th, and a fifteen days supply of water was obtained without a shot being fired. Previously they had been unable to show a finger outside the fort. Lieut. Vincent caused many casualties and on the 10th, when the relieving column from Kirghi advanced to the relief, hills were picketted under the protection of his machine, and in spite of the fact there were reported to have been anything from 2000 to 10000 Mahsuds in the surrounding hills, the relief was carried out without a shot being fired. Lieut. Vincent was the first to land on Jandola aerodrome, and entered the fort while the relieving troops were still a mile away.

In addition to this, reconnaissances were carried out with bomb raids, daily in the direction of Wana, the scene of the recent mutiny of the Wana militia, where the mutineers seized the posts of Wana, Sarawaki and Tanai, aided by the Wazirs and Mahsuds.

Between June 15th and 28th, Lieuts. Vincent and Curry carried out daily bombing and reconnaissance raids on Wana. On the first of Lieut. Vincent's raids, great surprise and moral effect was caused by gliding down from 6000 feet and dropping seven 20 lb. bombs in the fort, which was packed with men and animals, causing many casualties. This distance was the extreme limit for these machines as on several occasions they landed at Tank aerodrome with no petrol in the tanks. Operations of this description were carried out until the detachment was withdrawn on July 5th.

At this time a letter was received from Simla, enclosing a special order of the day, issued by Brigadier General N.D.K. MacEwan, to be read out on parade, to the following effect:-

"The General Officer Commanding, Royal Air Force, conveys to Officers and other ranks of the Royal Air Force, his high appreciation of the excellent work performed since the present operations commenced.

He realises the strenuous and difficult conditions under which the work and flying was carried out, which make the excellent work performed since the present operations commenced.

He realises the strenuous and difficult conditions under which the work and flying was carried out, which make the excellent results all the more creditable and which could only have been brought about by continuous and conscientious work on the part of the W.O's, N.C.O's, and A.C.M's, under very trying weather conditions.

He feels confident that the excellent spirit, so far shown will be maintained at that high pitch which has brought the name of the Royal Air Force to such a high level during the War".

In the first week in June, three machines were also detached to Bannu. These were later increased to six and periodical reconnaissances and bomb raids were carried out until the arrival of 20 Squadron early in September, when these machines returned to Risalpur.

This flight was originally intended to be the detached flight which had come from Aden to Risalpur in June 1919, and was actually part of 114 Squadron. The personnel changed so rapidly through sickness, heat etc., that in a very short time it consisted almost entirely of officers and men of 31 Squadron.

Incidents of note during this detachment were:- On June 30th, two Machines made a reconnaissance and dropped peace propaganda about Landa-Tor-Ni-Oba and Matun. Three old cannons opened fire on them from Matun and Lieut. Junor reported having seen the cannon balls flying through the air. It was easy to see the cannon firing from the ground as they had no recoil mechanism, and every time they fired they ran back for some distance raising large clouds of dust.

Early on July 14th a determined attack was made on Bannu aerodrome by local tribes. This attack was beaten off by the aerodrome guard, causing many casualties to the tribesmen. On the 16th their villages were bombed and burnt by the Infantry, in retaliation. Many bullet holes were found in the roof of the hangar and the Political Agent subsequently reported that the tribesmen had purposely fired into the roof of the hangar as they were under the impression that the machine would be roosting in the roof, or if not would be flying around in it as soon as flying commenced.

The history must now return to **Risalpur**, where the usual programme of training was being carried out. Flying had been curtailed in order that machines might be overhauled and personnel given a rest, pending possible heavy demands should hostilities recommence. All ranks that could not be spared were sent to the hills. At the same time the following airmen were selected to take part in the Peace Celebrations, and for Demobilization on extreme compassionate grounds. They left the Squadron on the 29th, Corporal J.W. Wintour, Corporal C.H. Stonebridge, A/C1. S.H. Coatsworth and A/C2. H.H. House.

On June 30th one machine was detailed to drop Proclamation Leaflets on Kahi and Peshbolak, but the machines had to return owing to engine trouble. Another machine was detailed to drop the leaflets on the villages between Hazarnac and Jallalabad. The pilot reported a big parade at Jallalabad of about a 1000 troops and 2000 civilians looking on, full dress uniform being worn. The pilot came down very low and dropped propaganda. The troops did not scatter but the civil population ran in all directions. When they saw that no hostile action was intended, they got quite excited and waved frantically, finally fighting among themselves for leaflets.

On the 20th Lieut. F.V. Devonshire was killed whilst on reconnaissance in the Chora area. His machine was completely wrecked. The following report of Lieut. Devonshire's death was received later from the Political Agent of the Khyber.

"Devonshire was flying very low over the retreating lashkar, causing considerable damage with his bombs and a great deal of confusion. As he passes from North to South across the plain close to Chora Fort, a single man stepped out from under a tree and had the extraordinary luck to hit Devonshire just below the right eyebrow and he must have been dead before reaching the ground. His body was unfortunately never recovered".

The above operations were commenced on September 13th, against Chora Fort in the Khyber District. Aeroplanes co-operated with Artillery and Infantry and carried out aerial offensive measures. The fort which was a very strong one, was built of stone and lime, and belonged to Yar Muhammed who had recently caused us considerable annoyance by harbouring outlaws etc. and by intriguing with Afghan Headquarters at Kabul. This was the first operation in which Bristol Fighters took part. During these operations a Bristol Fighter was forced to land in the Bazar Valley, and the pilot, Lieut. Wells and his observer Lieut. Winstanley were taken into captivity. They were however treated well and after negotiations were returned by the Zakka Khel Jirga. A heavy ransom was paid for them. A copy of Lieut. Wells report is given below. British and Indian troops arrived at the scene of the forced landing shortly after the occupants of the machine had been captured, and the bombs on the machine unfortunately exploded in their midst, resulting in six casualties to Indian other ranks.

Lieut. Wells report reads:- On the morning of the 13th, on my way to Chora, I flew over the hills to the South of the Bazar Valley in order to view the approaches from that side including the BARA Valley. The engine was running smoothly I heard a shot or two and later found boiling water coming back into my face. I glanced at the thermometer which registered well over boiling point. I immediately turned back being a little way West of Chora. Later smoke commenced to issue from the cowling and the engine dropped revs., eventually seizing up completely. I made up my mind to land in a green patch of cultivation about 1½ miles East of Chora. This was as far as I could glide, it turned out to be terraced and walled. Finding that I had slightly overshot I dipped my right wing to the ground. The undercarriage was swept off and the machine then rolled over to the right. Lieut. Winstanley was thrown out of the cockpit and landed on his shoulder, fortunately only bruising himself. Beyond this neither of us sustained any injuries. Winstanley immediately went to his cockpit to get a pigeon for release, he got hold of a pigeon box and his revolver, and had just turned away when a Pathan slipped in and relieved him of both. We then found about six to eight Pathans by our side. Their approach was entirely concealed by the maize. They pointed to a nullah just below us and said "Chelo". After crossing the nullah, in which there was a great deal of water, we went westwards. Our troops were fighting at the time with rifles and a Lewis gun. Winstanley told me later that a good number of bullets came very close to him. We got out of sight however and started to climb a hill but what was little more than a goat track. It was here that I came to grief by holding on to a piece of projecting rock. This turned out to be rotten and I fell about five feet on to a lot of scaly rock, tobogganing down some 50 feet, until I pulled up short on some boulders and bushes. I was a great deal bruised and sustained a rather deep cut on the knee. A Pathan who went down with me broke his collar bone. In the meantime Winstanley had been taken on ahead. I eventually rejoined him about midday. We continued to march until about 4 p.m. when we halted by a stream and had a meal, consisting of chuppatties and mutton, a dumba having been bought and killed. The warm skin was worn by the man with the broken collar bone for two days! At six o'clock we again moved, and after another three hours march we camped for the night. They gave us a thick woollen mat to sleep on and one man threw a greatcoat over me. Another dressed my cuts with hot ghee and salt.

The following morning we moved on at about 6.30 arriving at a summer camp at about 11 a.m. There were no buildings, only rude branch shelters. We were told that we were going no further. We remained until the evening of the 15th, when after a big Jirgah they removed Winstanley to the valley. I remained in the hills until the evening of the 18th, when I was also moved down, about 2½ hours march. The village in which Winstanley was, was pointed out to me, and turned out to be about 1½ miles from my show.

The Malika of the Khyber had been sent out by the Political Agent to arrange for our release. A settlement was finally come to on the morning of the 20th. Within an hour we were moving towards Landi Kotal. We put up in the village of Karamna or Karani and the following day arrived at Landi Kotal. During the whole of our time we were well treated by the tribesmen, many of them in fact being ex-soldiers, and moreover there was nearly always a Political messenger present from the morning of the 16th".

On the morning of October 10th, three machines left Risalpur for Bannu, to take part in a large raid on Dotanni Kot in the Wana plain. The officers taking part were Flight Lieut. Watts, Observer Officer Nicholson, Flying Officer Junor, Observer Officer Greenslade, Flying Officer Vincent and Observer Officer Hayward. The return flight from Bannu to Wana alone took $3\frac{1}{4}$ hours and some of the pilots glided the last few miles into Bannu aerodrome with no petrol left.

The machines which took part in this raid were:-

3 Machines from Bannu	(20 Squadron)	Bristol Fighters
4 Machines from Tank	(20 Squadron)	do.
3 Machines from Risalpur	(31 Squadron)	do.
1 Machine from Mianwali	(97 Squadron)	D.H.10s now 60 Sqdn.
5 Machines from Mianwali	(99 Squadron)	D.H. 9s now 27 Sqdn.

On November 26th three machines were despatched to Bannu to work with 20 Squadron, at the beginning of the operations against the Mahsuds in the Tank Zam Valley. They remained there until December 2nd, and carried out bomb raids and ground strafing in the neighbourhood of Marobi, Janjai, Makin and other villages. The officers were:- Flt. Lt. Watts, F/O Junor and F/O. O'Brien Saint and Observer Officers Wright and Godfrey.

The final event of the year was a Royal Air Force Sports week at Lahore, at which all who could possibly be spared were present. The sports cup was won by 31 Squadron.

The following officers were on the strength of the squadron during 1919:-

Capt.   D.H.M. Carberry, M.C.,D.F.C.
Capt.   C.E. Sherwin, M.C.
Capt.   W.J. Butler, A.F.C.
Capt.   F.J. Watts.
Capt.   G.W. Robartes.
Lieut. R.S. Greenslade.
Lieut. J.M. Godfrey.
Lieut. R.B. Dormer.
Lieut. C.J. Guthrie.
Lieut. C.S. McGregor.
Lieut. M.H. Findlay.
Lieut. M.R. D'Arcy.
Lieut. N.S. Paynter.
Lieut. C.Mc.C. Vincent.
Lieut. C.N. Ellen.
Lieut. W.J. Allen.
Lieut. A.S. Cox.
Lieut. G.L. Nicholson.
Lieut. G.L. Blake.
Lieut. F.C. Carter.
Lieut. N. Wright.
Lieut. G. Winstanley.
Lieut. J. Platt.
Lieut. H. Wisnnekowitz.
Lieut. R.C. Williams.

Lieut. J.T.O'Brien Saint.
Lieut. R.A. Curry.
Lieut. K.H. Brown.
Lieut. E.G.H. Ellis.
Lieut. F.E.E. Villiers.
Lieut. E.G. Keeping.
Lieut. P. Pipe.
Lieut. R.P.A. Crisp.
Lieut. T. Romney.
Lieut. L.C. Boyd.
Lieut. C.M. Eastley.
Lieut. A.L. Watkins.
Lieut. E.T.H. Hill.
Lieut. P. Murgatroyd.
Lieut. Oddie.
Lieut. Junor, D.F.C.
Capt. H.H. Thompson.
2/Lt. S.G. Davis.
2/Lt. J.E. Poraria.
2/Lt. P.G. Wills.
2/Lt. B.R. Harris.
2/Lt. S.R. Road.

The following officers were posted to the Squadron for 114 Squadron.

Capt. D.F. Murray.
2/Lt. S.F. Hodgson.
2/Lt. E.N. Henett.

The following officers were with the Squadron but were posted away before the end of 1919.

Capt. O. Hughes.
Lieut. G.G. Barker.
2/Lt. S. Moyles.
Lieut. R.C. Mullinger.
2/Lt. G.A. Body.
Lieut. R. Hayward.
2/Lt. N. Burke.
2/Lt. R.C. Williamson.
Lieut. J.L. Kirby.
Lieut. F.H. Whiteley.
2/Lt. E.T. Crosslet.
Capt. E.N. Ashton.
Lieut. C.S. Bellamy.
2/Lt. C.J. Hutton.
2/Lt. L.J. Hoare.
Lieut. R.M. Rankin.
Lieut. D.S. Liston.
Lieut. A.V. Gompertz.
Lieut. C.H. Thompson.
Capt. R.H. Shears.
2/Lt. G.P. White.

```
2/Lt.   J. Platt.
2/Lt.   W.F. Stewart.
2/Lt.   W.E. Neville.
Lieut.  E.H. King.
Lieut.  G.D. Longfellow.
Capt.   G.R. Travis.
Major   E.L. Millar, M.B.E.
Lieut.  H.D. Scowcroft.
Lieut.  F.C. Devonshire (Killed in action)
Lieut.  W.T. Frazer.
Lieut.  D. Rooke.
Lieut.  J. Morrel.
Lieut.  K.H. Brown.
Capt.   R.L. Thoms.
2/Lt.   W.B.E. Fetherstone.
2/Lt.   F.G. White.
Capt.   D. Halley, D.F.C.
```

1 9 2 0

At the commencement of 1920, the Squadron was still at Risalpur, and "A" Flight under Flight Lieut. Watts was still on detachment with 20 Squadron at Bannu. This detachment was employed in carrying out a considerable amount of photography, reconnaissance and bombing in connection with the Mahsud Operations. The detachment lasted six weeks and the Flight then returned to Risalpur.

Towards the beginning of the year there were many changes in the personnel of the Squadron. Command was taken over by Squadron Leader A.D. Neale, M.C. from Squadron Leader D.H.M. Carberry, M.C.,D.F.C., who had been in temporary command. The Squadron also contained many temporary Officers who had been retained for the Afghan and Mahsud operations and who had not been granted either permanent or short service commissions, these were now sent home for demobilisation as quickly as transport became available. Other Officers went to home establishment either on leave or posting, and large numbers of reliefs for all ranks, arrived from home.

The usual programme of training was commenced both of ground and flying, the latter being carried out on Bristol Fighters, and on two Avros with 110 Le Rhone engines. The Squadron was now entirely equipped with Bristol Fighters as their service machine, and early in February, Flying Officer K.E. Ward flew the last B.E.2e with 90 R.A.F. engine to Lahore. Much time was occupied in building the new Bristols, many of which were sent to 20 Squadron at Bannu to replace machines crashed or lost in the Mahsud operations. At the same time large numbers of the Squadron's personnel of all ranks were posted away to "A" Squadron which was forming at the time.

On January 17th, as a result of the Operations at the end of 1919, in which the squadron took part, the following telegram was received:-

"The Waziristan Force Commander has seen with the greatest pleasure General Skeen's recognition of the work done by the Royal Air Force. Your work must have reached a high standard of excellence, and he is sure that the recognition of this by the Infantry, whom you are assisting so greatly, will recompense you for all the heavy calls to which you have always responded so readily and effectively".

On January 27th, another telegram was received from Wing Commander F.S. Minchin on his relinquishing command of the 52nd Wing:-

"Wing Commander F.S. Minchin wishes to thank all officers, N.C.O's and men for their loyal and wholehearted co-operation during the 3rd Afghan War, and the Waziristan Expedition. The concerted efforts of all units have materially affected the results of both these campaigns, and their value is fully appreciated by the higher Army and Air Force Authorities."

On February 23rd, the following message was received from Air Marshall Sir H.M. Trenchard, Bart.,K.C.B.,D.S.O., Chief of the Air Staff, to the Royal Air Force in India:-

"Hearty congratulations to all ranks on satisfactory reports of operations and maintenance of R.A.F. units on Indian Frontier".

In March, orders were received for the Squadron to move to Mhow in April. The whole Squadron left by rail on April 13th, taking with them only three Bristol Fighters. The move was accomplished with two trains, and was completed in two days in spite of the fact that the Bristols had to be packed in B.E. cases, and that machines, stores and troops had to be transhipped at Rutlam on to the narrow gauge railway. The transport completed the journey from Rutlam to Mhow by road.

As far as the Aerodrome and Quarters were concerned Mhow was not a success. The Officers mess was a mile from the Barracks and the Aerodrome was two miles from either of them. The Aerodrome was composed of black cotton soil, which became soft and boggy in wet weather.

Soon after arrival four R.A.F. hangars were erected and work on the machines was started.

The Squadron then commenced flying training along the usual lines. The flying caused great excitement among the natives, as an aeroplane had never been seen before in that part of India. For months afterwards whether there was any flying or not, there was always a large crowd of Indians squatting round the aerodrome.

One more machine arrived with the rear party, making the total strength of the machine up to four. No further machines arrived till September, when four more were received.

About this time an interesting flight was carried out by Flying Officer Cummings, with Flying Officer Ellen as observer. The occasion was a review of his troops by the Maharaja of Dhar. The machine arrived at Dhar while the parade was in progress, and did a little stunting, finally flying low along the parade ground and saluting the Maharaja. On another occasion a machine landed at Dhar at the Maharaja's invitation and was inspected by him and his household. Shortly afterwards, Squadron Leader Neale and three other Officers were invited to dinner by him, when a silver cup was presented to the Officers of the Squadron and another to Squadron Leader Neale, to commemorate the occasion of the first aeroplane to fly over Dhar.

It had been understood all along that the move to Mhow was to be a temporary one, and that Cawnpore was to be the permanent station of the Squadron. For this reason both the Officers' and Sergeants' Messes existed as far as possible on what could be hired locally. In spite of this the Officers' Mess in the old Cavalry Bungalow and the Sergeants' Mess in the Connaught Barracks, were made very comfortable.

In June of this year a new rate of pay was brought in to force for officers serving in the Royal Air Force in India. On reading the official pamphlet on the subject, one was led to believe that owing to the "increased cost of living" the new rates would be beneficial to all officers. On the rates being published, it was found that all except the most senior officers, had suffered to the extent of Rs.100 or more, with the exception of Observers, who were now, quite rightly, to be paid the same as pilots. Married junior officers were now in a desperate plight, and it was not until the end of 1921 that a marriage allowance was even rumoured in the country. The adjustment of the new rates of pay resulted in renewed and intensive hostilities with the D.D.O. which, as the records show, had commenced soon after the Squadron had arrived in India in 1915.

The days of many and varied uniforms came to an end about the middle of the year. The Service Dress and Mess uniforms were finally settled and officers were ordered to obtain these by the end of December. The pattern of Tropical Mess kit was changed from the open pea-jacket with the light blue cummerbund and dark blue shoulder straps, to the "old cavalry pattern" jacket with white waistcoat and shoulder straps. The shoulder straps were later changed back to dark blue with gold badges of rank.

On the Ninth of July the London Gazette published the following extract:-

"His Majesty the King has been graciously pleased to give orders for the following promotion and appointment to the Most Excellent Order of the British Empire, in recognition of distinguished services:-

To be a member of the Military Division of the said most excellent order:-

Observer Officer Albert John Cox. 31 Squadron R.A.F.

"His Majesty the King has been graciously pleased to approve of the undermentioned rewards for gallantry and distinguished services:-

Awarded the Distinguished Flying Cross.
Flying Officer Gerald Stephen Oddie. 31 Squadron.
Flying Officer Claude McLean Vincent. 31 Squadron."

About September of this year all Observers were sent either to the Middle East or to Home Establishment for flying instruction and the Squadron now had fewer officers on the strength than ever before.

Orders were received about August that the Squadron was to move to Cawnpore in October, and the work of the four new machines was accelerated, the last one being completed a few days before the Squadron left for Cawnpore. The machines left on November 26th, in two flights of four machines each on two subsequent days and landings were made at Hoshangabad, Bina, Jhansi, and lastly, Cawnpore, a distance of about 600 miles. Seven of the machines completed the journey without any trouble, the eighth flown by Squadron Leader Neale forced landed near Hoshangabad with magneto trouble, but got off successfully and arrived at Cawnpore two days later.

Special landing grounds were prepared at Hoshangabad and Bina for this flight in addition to several intermediate forced landing grounds. The arrangements for the supply of petrol and oil were made by the Supply and Transport Corps.

The following were the pilots of the machines which made this flight:-

> Squadron Leader Neale
> Flight Lieutenant Watts
> Flight Lieutenant Thompson
> Flight Officer Cummings
> Flight Officer Paynter
> Flying Officer Vincent
> Flying Officer Ward
> Flying Officer Williamson-Jones.

On arrival at Cawnpore the Squadron occupied Nos. 8, 9 and 10 bungalows of the Wheeler Barracks. No.8 Barrack was of interest in view of the fact that during the Indian Mutiny it formed part of the defences under a Lieutenant Thompson. The Aerodrome was on the old racecourse and was of generous proportions; the Officers' Mess was in No.48 Bungalow and several of the officers had their bungalows on the banks of the Ganges.

Shortly after arrival at Cawnpore the Squadron was again brought up to strength by the arrival of four more machines from Aircraft Park, Lahore. They came by air via Ambala, Delhi and Agra, and were flown by Flying Officers Cummings, Robinson, Oddie and Paynter, arriving on December 18th.

With regard to sport, the Squadron Association Football team was a sound, all round side. Many good Squadron and interflight matches were played, during the year, the most notable being in the Mhow Divisional Cup Competition, when the match between the Squadron and the 3rd Battn. K.R.R.'s had to be played three times before a result could be obtained, and the third match was lost by one goal scored in the last minute of the game. In a combined team of 28 and 31 Squadron Players chosen to play in the Durand Cup Competition at Simla, a large percentage of 31 Squadron Players were chosen.

Rugby Football was taken up by most of the Officers during the monsoon and matches were played against the K.R.R.'s and the Gymkhana Club with considerable success.

Several Cricket matches were played, the most amusing being one between the Officers and other Ranks. The men batted first and were all out for 37, and the result looked like an easy win for the officers. The officers then went in and succeeded in making a total of 25, the highest score being made by an officer who had never played cricket before.

Two race meetings were held while the Squadron was at Mhow, and on both occasions Flight Lieut. Watts' "Tarsan" won the two miles flat race at long odds, and the same horse was third in the steeplechase in the last meeting after having refused a jump.

Polo was played regularly by four or five Officers but a high enough standard to raise a team was never reached.

Several Hockey matches were played and a billiard tournament was played on the Institute tables which was keenly fought out, in spite of the uneveness of the tables, and was won by one of the Headquarters Flight Teams.

The shooting in the neighbourhood of Mhow was fairly good, and at the invitations of the Maharajas of Indore and Dhar, several expeditions after buck were made and oome good heads obtained. Snipe, duck and sand grouse, were plentiful and large bags were frequently brought to the Mess.

The yearly competition for the Slaley Revolver Shooting Cup was held in June, and was won by Flight Lieut. T.F.W. Thompson, and the subsequent ceremony, as laid down in the rules for the competition, was carried out in the Mess a few days later.

The following Officers were on the strength of the Squadron at the end of 1920.

Headquarter Flight.

Sqdn.Ldr.	A.L. Neale, M.C.	
F/Lt.	J.F. Hosford.	Medical Officer.
F/O.	R.B. Dormor.	Armament Officer.
F/O.	G.G.C. Huggard.	
F/O.	F.G.A. Robinson.	
F/O.	G.M. Whitton.	Wireless Officer.
F/O.	W.M. Long.	Adjutant.

"A" Flight.

F/Lt.	F.J. Watts.
F/O.	P.H. Davy.
F/O.	H.R. Junor, D.F.C.
F/O.	G.S. Oddie, D.F.C.

"B" Flight.

F/Lt.	J.C.O. Dickson, D.F.C.
F/O.	N.S. Paynter.
F/O.	C.Mc.C. Vincent, D.F.C.
F/O.	E.A.J. Brown.

"C" Flight.

F/Lt.	T.F.W. Thompson.
F/O.	K.E. Ward.
F/O.	R.A. Vosper.
F/O.	J.D. Jackson.

---

1 9 2 1

The first event of interest was the arrival of Squadron Leader A.T. Harris, A.F.C. who took over command from Flight Lieut. Neale, M.C., who had reverted from Squadron Leader, being too young, under the new regulations to retain his rank.

The Squadron was now equipped with its full peace time establishment of twelve Bristol Fighters, i.e. four per flight. Advantage was now taken of the cold weather to commence training, which consisted of puff shoots, bombing, camera gun practice, photography, and flying tests, as laid down in full in A.M.W.O's.

The ground training consisted in Gunnery and lectures on many and varied subjects, leading up to a written examination in March.

In January "C" Flight flew to Jhansi to take part in a ten days Artillery Practice Camp. The pilots were Flight Lieut. Thompson, F/O. Ward, F/O. Vosper, F/O. Robinson, and F/O. Jackson, Flying Officer Whitton went with the flight as Wireless Officer. Shoots with live shell were carried out daily and much was learned by both arms. The flight returned ten days later without mishap, a reconnaissance for sites for landing grounds having been carried out on both the outward and return journeys. The distance from Cawnpore to Jhansi is about 150 miles.

At the Duke of Connaught's Durbar at Delhi in January, the Royal Air Force provided a Guard of Honour of three Officers and one hundred other ranks. The Officers were Squadron Leader Mackay, Flight Lieut. Coryton, M.V.O., and F/O. G. Randaoo, D.F.C. The squadron provided about thirty men for this party.

Air Commodore T.I. Webb-Bowen was personally congratulated by the Duke of Connaught on the smartness and turnout of this bodyguard.

In February, the Squadron was inspected by Field Marshall Lord Rawlinson, Commander-in-Chief in India. On this occasion the Squadron did not parade with the rest of the troops on the station, but was drawn up in front of the machines on the aerodrome.

The visit of the C. in C. was the beginning of a great economy campaign throughout all arms in India. This was carried out to such an extent that it was with great difficulty that machines were kept serviceable. On one occasion a machine was flown with rope on one side of the axle instead of shock absorber, as this was unobtainable in the country and machines had to be returned as unserviceable owing to lack of split pins.

In order to comply with A.M.W.O's. for the winter training, all pilots who had not taken part in the flight from Mhow, had to carry out at least one cross country flight. The route selected was from Cawnpore to Agra, with a landing at Etawah, a distance of about 150 miles each way. This flight was carried out by Flight Lieut. Coryton, and F/O's. Junor, Jackson and Davy. Shortly after this F/O. Jackson ferried a machine from Amballa to Cawnpore to replace one previously crashed. He experienced considerable trouble on this flight having two forced landings from magneto trouble, which necessitated changing both magnetos at Delhi.

At the end of February two machines flew to Lucknow to demonstrate at a meeting which was being addressed by Mr. Ghandi, the leader of the Non-Co-operation Party. The machines, acting under the instructions of the civil authorities, circled over the meeting and dropped pamphlets containing the Duke of Connaught's speech. It was ascertained afterwards that the machines attracted far more interest than Mr. Ghandi's speech and he had considerable difficulty in making himself heard above the roar of the engines.

In April with the beginning of the hot weather the first party left for the R.A.F. hill station at Lower Barian Murree. It consisted of "B" Flight and one third of Headquarters Flight. Two Officers accompanied this party and the many and complicated arrangements for moving the troops in the Indian hot weather were successfully carried out. At the same time the leave season opened.

The Summer Training Programme now came into force. It consisted of all the usual flying training practices and had to be carried out fortnightly by all pilots. Experiments were also carried out with the High Angle drift sight, and a great controversy arose as to whether it should be used by the pilot or the observer.

In June shoots were organised with 117 Battery R.A.F. using old 15 pounder guns, on the banks of the Ganges. These were carried out with considerable success, but had to be abandoned later, owing to the rise of the river, which completely covered the practice area. These shoots provided excellent practice in the drill of both arms, but the O.K.'s recorded were more frequently due to a homing instinct on the part of the pilot, than to good shooting or accurate observation, as the guns, ammunition and sights had been condemned as unserviceable, many years before.

In June the second party went to Lower Barian, and the first party returned. Owing to the anticipated move of the Squadron to Peshawar, expected to take place in September, a further party of 15 airmen were sent on medical recommendation to the hills, as the last party had been cancelled.

The heat towards the beginning of the monsoon became intense, and an unusual number of cases of heat stroke were recorded. In spite of this fact, the Squadron escaped without a single case, although the temperature for several weeks remained in the neighbourhood of 120 degrees in the shade.

On July 21st, F/O E.G. Keeping, left the Squadron for Bombay in order to get married before leaving India on a transfer to Home Establishment. This officer was one of the oldest members of the Squadron, having joined them in Risalpur in 1917.

On July 25th, a cooling system test was carried out with the Rolls Royce engine, the machine being flown "all out" up to 10,000 feet. The time taken to attain this height, complete with passenger, 40 lbs of ballast, and wireless set, was $17\frac{1}{2}$ minutes. The water boiled from 3,000 feet to 5,000 feet, the total loss being 14 pints. No trouble developed during flight.

The monsoon now started in earnest, and an extract from a summary of information, shows the state of the ground at this time. "Dummy bombing has been temporarily suspended, in order that a few derelict bombs may be retrieved from the mud, into which they disappeared some days ago.

Soon after the commencement of the rain rugby football started, in spite of the temperature which was well over 100 degrees in the shade. The Squadron turned out a surprisingly strong team, which defeated the Cawnpore Sports Club, in frequently repeated games. The games were played in ten minute "chukkers", on account of the heat.

On August 22nd, the last detachment arrived from the hills, bringing with them the Drill and Sports Cup which they had won. In the Cross Country Race, the Squadron team of six men took the 1st, 2nd, 4th, 11th and 14th places.

To celebrate this event, an excellent dinner and smoking concert was organised by the remainder of the Squadron at which the Cups were formally taken over.

Towards the middle of September, the Summer flying training programme had to be curtailed, owing to the preliminary arrangements for the move to Peshawar.

At this time the Squadron Rugger team went to Allahabad for the week-end to play the Station. The Squadron was beaten by 24 points to nil, but the game was much more even than the score indicated. The officers were entertained very enthusiastically at the Club, whilst the men were the guests of the 1st Battalion of the Black Watch.

From now onwards the preparations for the move to Peshawar, occupied everyone's time. Machines were made serviceable and beautified, stores were packed, train and landing ground arrangements were started, and the advanced party was sent off.

Before leaving a farewell dinner and dance was given by the members of the Cawnpore Club, to the Officers of the Squadron. The evening was a great success, and many touching, but slightly bemused speeches of farewell were made. The sergeants also gave a farewell dance at the King Edward's Memorial Hall, at which no time or energy was spared by them to make the evening a complete success.

The first formation left Cawnpore on October 15th for Peshawar. The pilots were Flt. Lieut. Watts and Coryton and F/O's. Vosper, Robinson, Jackson and Playford.

The machines had all been tuned up, repainted and generally beautified, and the formation left the ground at 6.30 a.m., and met with nothing but misfortune during the whole of their trip. At Agra at the end of the first stage F/O Vosper had the misfortune to overshoot the aerodrome and turn the machine on its nose, but was luckily not seriously injured. F/Lt. Watts was also delayed there several days with a broken fuselage fitting. The remainder of the formation reached Delhi the same afternoon, and were entertained by the Leicester Regiment, to a guest night.

Next morning the formation left for Amballa in a rainstorm, and in the afternoon ran into a duststorm near Lahore, which was of such intensity that it was impossible to see the ground from over three hundred feet and then only by following the railway could the pilots find their way to Lahore. F/O's Robinson and Jackson missed the railway and were forced to land on the first available open space. F/O Jackson landed in a recreation ground and crashed, whilst F/O Robinson landed in a field of maize and managed to get off again the next morning, and landed at Lahore. This stout effort on the part of F/O Robinson saved the dismantling of the machine and the delay of the formation.

F/Lt. Coryton and F/O Playford continued the journey alone the next morning and arrived safely, via Jhelum that afternoon.

The second formation consisting of F/Lt. Thompson and F/O's. Vincent, Oddie, Junor and Morston, left on the morning of the 16th. F/O Vincent forced landed twice between Cawnpore and Agra, but arrived there before the formation left, and followed two days later. The rest of the formation met with no difficulties, picked up F/O Robinson at Lahore and arrived at Peshawar in safety, although two machines had to wait at Risalpur for two or three days, until sufficient hangars were erected at Peshawar for their accommodation.

The personnel, stores and all ground sections moved up in two trains, and arrived without a hitch after a journey of 48 hours. The troops were met at the station by the band of the West Yorkshire Regiment and were marched into barracks.

No sooner had the Squadron arrived than a detachment flight were ordered to Akora, for an Artillery practice Camp, where the benefits derived from the intensive summer training were found to be of the greatest assistance. "B" Flight was detailed for this duty, and proceeded there under the command of F/Lt. Coryton, M.V.O. The whole camp was most interesting and gradually as the Gunners began to get used to the new procedure which had just been brought out for use in unmapped country, and the co-operation became closer, improvements and suggestions were evolved and tried. At the end of the camp a combined report was submitted by Wing Commander W.G.S. Mitchell, D.S.O.,M.C.,A.F.C., and Colonel Curling, M.B.E.,R.A., which reflect great credit on the Squadron. In addition to this camp, many contact patrol practices were carried out with the Infantry at Jalozai, Jamrud and Nowshera, and shoots were also carried out with the pack batteries at Jamrud.

The year finished with the usual Christmas Festivities and short leave.

The following Officers were on the strength of the Squadron at the end of 1921:-

Headquarter Flight.

Sqn.Ldr.	A.T. Harris, A.F.C.	
F/O.	G.M.W. Whitton.	Wireless Officer.
F/O.	W.M. Long.	Adjutant.
F/O.	W.N. Lancaster.	
F/O.	H.R. Junor, D.F.C.	Armament Officer.
F/O.	R.B. Dormer.	Medical Officer.
F/Lt.	H.Mc.W. Daniels.	Stores Officer.
F/O.	R.S. Smyth, M.C.	

"A" Flight.

F/Lt.	F.J. Watts.
F/O.	T.K. Breakell.
F/O.	N.V. Moreton.
F/O.	L.H. Ridley.

"B" Flight.

F/Lt.	W.A. Coryton, M.V.O.
F/O.	E.R.B. Playford.
F/O.	E.A.J. Brown.
F/O.	C.Mc.C. Vincent, D.F.C.
F/O.	E. Chadwick Brown.

"C" Flight.

F/Lt.	T.W.F. Thompson.
F/O.	A.B. Ellwood, D.S.C.
F/O.	F.G.A. Robinson.
F/O.	J.D. Jackson.
F/O.	A. Ledger.

1 9 2 2

In January and February, "A" and "C" Flights took their turns at the practice camp at Akora, where the experiments carried out on the first camp were perfected, until by the end of the training season all pilots in the Squadron were able to handle all types of shoots, and the speed with which pilots were now able to direct the Gunners on to the targets, clearly showed the value of co-operation in unmapped country.

A large amount of Infantry co-operation was also carried out, even in the mountainous districts of the Khyber with the greatest success. The Director Arrow, the Popham Panel, and Wireless were brought into play for this purpose, and owing to the great keenness and energy of the Officers of the Squadron, led by the O.C., Squadron Leader A.T. Harris, A.F.C., the other services were gradually convinced of the enormous value of the assistance which could be rendered by aeroplane co-operation. On one occasion an aeroplane Machine Gunning and Bombing demonstration was given before an Indian Battalion which astonished them greatly. On another occasion during a contact patrol show near Nowshera, the Officer Commanding the Column with which the aeroplane was co-operating received so much information as to the enemies dispositions and his own troops progress, in the form of situation maps that he exclaimed, "How many more of these is he going to drop"?.

On the return of the last Flight from Akora, the Officers were plunged into the thick of the yearly examinations which included every possible subject, and caused many searchings of heart, and many evening lectures. However, the Squadron did very creditably, in spite of the fact that owing to the absence of the flight at Akora, very little preparation could be made.

During the cold weather, Peshawar proved to be an excellent station for sport, the Rugby and Association Teams both doing extremely well, although both were weakened by the loss of Officers and posted to Home Establishment. Hunting with the P.V.H., Polo, Golf, Tennis, etc., combined with excellent Snipe and Duck shooting were taken advantage of by the Squadron. The best snipe bag in one day being twenty five couples to two guns.

In the Peshawar district "Point to Point", the Officers of the Peshawar District R.A.F., gained 5th, 6th and 9th places. F/O Elwood, the only representative of the Squadron came in 8th.

In the annual Sports Meeting held at Amballa during March, the Individual Cup, for the best all round athlete, presented by the Maharaja of Patiala was shared by A/C Weeks with one of No.27 Squadron, the cup to be held for half the year by each squadron. The Royal Air Force Individual Cup was also won by this airman.

On March 4th, H.R.H. the Prince of Wales paid a visit to Peshawar. The personnel of the Squadron helped to line the streets on his arrival, and a formation of five machines met his train outside Nowshere station and escorted it into Peshawar and then circled round over head until H.R.H. entered Government House.

On the 6th, H.R.H. inspected the Pensioners in the Native City, personnel of the Squadron again lining the streets and a formation of three machines escorted him until the inspection was completed. On the 7th, the Prince at a General Inspection of troops in the Station expressed a desire to see the Royal Air Force informally at the completion of the parade. The Officers and Men waited for him by their machines which were drawn up for his inspection outside the hangars. All Officers were presented, and an amusing incident occurred when H.R.H. spoke to F/Lt. Coryton, M.V.O. The Prince asked him where he got his M.V.O., and Coryton replied that he got it for teaching H. R. H. the Duke of York to fly. The Prince replied "Good Lord"! fancy not remembering your face. I must write and tell Bertie about this".

On the occasion of the practice for the Prince of Wales Review the Squadron, being the junior service marched past last, and it so happened that they came directly behind the mules of the S & T.C. The Squadron marched past at a little greater distance than that laid down in regulations and the matter was noticed and mentioned by District Headquarters after the parade, when the infuriated senior Air Force Officer is understood to have stated that the next time they would march twice the distance behind, and would be armed with dust pans and brushes.

During the Prince of Wales visit there were several dances and a garden party at Government House, to which the Officers were invited.

The Prince left Peshawar on the night of the 7th and the time of his departure was supposed to be a secret. However at dinner that night, which happened to be a Guest Night, word was passed round that the train was leaving at 21.45 hours, and that transport was being provided for any officer that wished to go to the station. A great send-off was given to H.R.H. who evidently appreciated it thoroughly, and the last that was seen of the Royal Train as it passed down the platform was an Airman running alongside offering his hand to the Prince and saying "put it there Sir" which H.R.H. did.

On the escort formation several photographs were taken of the Royal Train, and the processions, and copies were presented to H.R.H. before his departure.

During the early part of the Winter a Jazz Band was formed. A magnificent start was given to it by the generous presentation of a trap drum outfit by Wing Commander W.G.S. Mitchell, D.S.O.,M.C.,A.F.C., the rest of the instruments were bought out of subscriptions from the Officers. The Band performed with great success at many dances at Peshawar Club.

On the 9th, all serviceable machines in the Squadron proceeded to Tank, in conjunction with 28 Squadron, on a raid on the Jalal Khel Wazire. The Squadron left at 06.00 hours in the morning and flew to Tank, did the bombing raid and returned to Peshawar the same day, arriving at dusk. The country was very mountainous and the targets bad, but bombs were dropped on flocks and villages, and a large number of rounds of ammunition fired.

This tribe had been causing considerable trouble by raiding Convoys and sniping in the Tank Zam District.

On the night of March 10th, orders were received about midnight for machines to fly to Tank, as the Khassidars holding Kajuri Kach Fort were being besieged. Four machines left at dawn, picked up the Political Agent at Tank and flew to the Fort. It was found that the besiegers had left. No action was taken and the machines were returned to Tank, filled up with petrol, and flew home to Peshawar the same evening. The distance from Peshawar to Tank is 180 miles.

On the 16th, H.E. The Viceroy paid an official visit to Peshawar, during which he inspected all the troops in the station together with Field Marshal Lord Rawlinson. The latter inspected the Squadron at work later in the morning, as it had not attended the general parade owing to the fact that all hands were hard at work preparing for operations at Dardoni.

On the morning of the 2nd of April, all available machines in the Squadron left for Dardoni, to take part in operations against the Ahmed Zai Wazirs, who had recently made an attempt on the life of the Political Agent of the Tochi, and were then threatening the line of communication between Dardoni and Datta Khel.

An intensive bombing by all the machines in the 1st Wing was planned, but owing to the fact that the local Thessildar had that day been captured by the enemy and was being held up for ransom, and that they also threatened to kill him if the bombing was commenced, the operations were cancelled by Lord Rawlinson, who was visiting Dardoni at the time. The machines accordingly returned to Peshawar on the 4th. F/O Moreton forced landed on the way home, near the entrance of the Kohat Pass, but the machine was undamaged and was salved the same day.

On the evening of the 6th, when the Officers of the Squadron were in the thick of a dance at the Club, at which the Squadron Jazz Band was playing, orders were suddenly received to the effect that the squadron would fly to Tank at dawn on the following day, for further operations. Preparations for this went on the whole night, and the band kept on until four o'clock in the morning, when the officers who had been playing had just time enough to get back, change, and reach the aerodrome in time to load up their machines and get away.

The object of the operations was to relieve the Political Thessildar, who with a handful of Khassidars was besieged by a large number of tribesmen in Wana Fort. These Khassidars were a newly-formed body of Irregulars, recruited from the local tribes, as an experiment in a new method of administering the Frontiers Tribes, and it was essential that every support should be given them immediately in order to ensure that they would not revert to type and go back to their friends the enemy.

The Squadron consisting of seven machines arrived at Tank at 09.00 hours, and started on the first raid at 13.00 hours. The leading machine carried the Political Agent of the Wana District, Major Parsons, for the purpose of communicating with the fort by means of message bags and ground strips, and for indicating targets to other machines.

The Formation arrived over Wana in the midst of a severe hailstorm, which stripped the propellors and the leading edges of the planes, and rendered operations impossible until it had passed over.

Excellent targets were found in the form of encampments and flocks on the open plains surrounding Wana and owing to the open nature of the country and the complete lack of cover, excellent results were obtained.

Towards the end of the raid the machine piloted by F/O Chadwick Brown, with F/O Jackson as observer forced landed owing to engine trouble near Wana Fort, and was observed by Sqd.Ldr. A.T. Harris, A.F.C., who was flying as observer to F/Lt. W.A. Coryton, M.V.O. He came down low and after dropping a message giving as much information as possible, escorted the two Officers until they were seen to be in the hands of Khassidars.

The following is the pilots report:-

"Arrived Wana 14.55, and dropped eight 20lb. bombs on encampments and flocks to the west of Wana Fort, at the foot of the hills. Three direct hits observed, the 4th bomb failed to explode. Then came down to 800 feet and fired 100 rounds of Lewis gun ammunition at flocks of sheep in the same vicinity. The Starboard side of the engine then cut right out, and the revs dropped to 1250. I headed for Wana Fort, believing it to be safe to land on the aerodrome within 50 yards of the fort, but was forced to land about 2 miles to the West. We immediately came under fire so abandoned the machine and ran for the fort. After we had gone for about five minutes, one of the machines spotted us, and coming down to within about 50 feet, dropped a message on us in a piece of 'four by two' weighted by an orange, telling us that the fort was straight in front of us and finishing up by saying 'run like hell'. Two men then came up on horseback making friendly signs, and making us mount their horses, led us to a ruined rifle butt near the fort. Wazirs then commenced coming in from all directions, firing, and the men with us whom we now understood to be Khassidars, and who had come from the fort to our rescue upon seeing us land, returned the fire.

Two more Khassidars now joined us, and mounting their horses we made a dash for the hills, closely followed by between 50 and 60 of the enemy. This was the only course we could have taken, as it was subsequently proved that the fort was closely invested, and as we could not have possibly got in, the Khassidars, by their prompt action saved us.

After we had gone about three miles, F/O Jackson's horse was hit in the hind quarters, causing him to ride and run, until another horse was obtained from a Khassidar that we met further on. We galloped for about fifteen miles into the hills and were continuously sniped until we managed to shake off the enemy on the top of a high ridge. We rode for another 25 miles until dusk when we had to get off and walk.

We had forced landed at about 15.30 hours, and we rode and walked through the mountains without stopping until 2330 hours. The route taken led us over the Lorelai Pass and round past Kanigaram. At 23.30 hours we pulled up for three hours in the house of a Mahsud Malik, and were treated with the utmost respect and kindness, and were given eggs, meat and tea.

At 02.30 hours we started off again and got within about five miles of Ladha, where we waited in a cave until dawn, as the Khassidars would not approach the camp in the dark for fear of the sentries, who had a nasty habit of shooting first and challenging afterwards. As soon as it was light we started off again and reached Ladha Camp at 07.00 hours, where we were most hospitably entertained by the Brigade, until the next day, when we proceeded by easy stages down to Tank Zam river, which was now in flood after the heavy hailstorm of the previous day, to Tank".

On the following day there were two raids, on both of which excellent targets were found. The admitted casualties obtained through the Political Agent for these and the previous raid were 11 men and 406 head of cattle, camels and sheep. On these raids the hostile encampments were seen to be moving farther and farther into the hills.

On the 9th, one raid was carried out, but few targets were found and the Political Agent decided to land at Wana the next morning if possible.

On the 10th, four machines flew to Wana, with the Political Agent in the leading machine. After dropping messages and receiving signals from the fort that all was clear, this machine landed, shortly afterwards signalling to the other machines to land as well. A jirga was held on the spot, and a reward of Rs.15,000 was distributed as a reward for the rescue of F/O's Brown and Jackson, the Khassidars having completed the return journey from Ladha on the evening of the 7th. The machines then returned to Tank.

On the 11th, another raid was carried out on the Bhomai Plain, to which the raiders had retreated. Small targets were found. A D.H.9a from Risalpur forced landed and crashed on Wana aerodrome, and a Bristol fighter from 28 Squadron also forced landed there.

Machines landed and brought away the pilot and observer of the D.H.9a whilst the crew of the Bristol being unable to get away spent the night in Wana Fort. As they were also unable to get away the next morning, they were picked up by other machines and the two engines were left in the fort. As the machines were all in a very bad condition a day was spent working on them, before returning to Peshawar.

Owing to the shortage of spares and the age of the machines, the Squadron was now decreasing in strength on account of the many engine failures and forced landings, and this became so acute that paragraphs appeared in the papers about it and questions were also raised in the House about it, only to be answered in the usual manner of present day politicians.

About the 22nd it was decided to reinforce Wana Fort with a detachment of the newly formed South Western Scouts, and two machines of the Squadron under F/O Ellwood, D.S.C., flew to Tank to co-operate with machines of 28 Squadron for the purpose of escorting this force and its convoy to Wana.

This march took five days, and a machine was kept overhead during the whole time that the column was on the move. No opposition was encountered in spite of the fact that a large force of enemy were reported to be gathering. This was probably due to the moral effect caused by the presence of the machines.

On the 6th day, when the column arrived at Wana, machines landed there with fitters, who dismantled the engines of the machines which had forced landed during the siege of Wana, and the dismantled parts were loaded on camels and brought to Tank. The machines returned to Peshawar the following day.

This concluded the Wana operations. During these the O.C. Squadron flew on every raid in the back seat of F/Lt. Coryton's machine, saying that he obtained more enjoyment out of using the Lewis Gun than out of bombing. F/O Vincent, D.F.C., with F/O Junor, D.F.C., received especial mention in the report of the operations, for good general work.

On May 6th, the Squadron moved to the hill station of Parachinnar, leaving behind a detachment of two flights under Flt/Lt. Thompson. Parachinnar takes it's name from a famous Chenar Tree under which Lord Roberts held a jirga (Conference) during his advance from Thal to Kabul and it is now the headquarters of the famous Kurram Militia.

During June, Pilot Officer G. Combe arrived. He was the first product of the R.A.F. Cadet College at Cranwell to come to the Squadron. Whilst he was being given landings on Peshawar aerodrome, by F/O Vincent, D.F.C., an amusing incident occurred. A mounted Infantry Major, ignoring the hoisted red flag, cantered on to the aerodrome, and began to cross it. The ever vigilant Officer of the Watch at once fired a Verey Light at him, of which he took no notice. But retribution was not slow in coming. F/O Vincent saw him and dived on him at speed. The Major at once broke into a gallop, but even so he bore the brunt of three more attacks.

1 9 2 2 - 1 9 2 3

In May 1922, Squadron Leader A.C. Maund, C.B.E.,D.S.O., took over command of the Squadron, which was equipped with Bristol Fighters and based at PESHAWAR. All remained quiet on the North West Frontier, until August when, from the twelfth onwards, almost daily bombing sorties were made against the militant tribesmen. Apart from this fortnight of sustained offensive activity, normal service training was carried out until April 1923, when a move was made to DARDONI in Waziristan.

Here the Squadron operated in close support of the army units engaged in quelling the sporadic uprisings of native tribes. All types of army co-operation duties were carried out, from the transporting of the G.O.C. Wazirforce to SARWEKAI and back again - a journey taking only two hours by air, as against three days by surface means - to the bombing of PRANG (rather aptly named) by ten machines on the 23rd of September. On this occasion the bombs dropped numbered twenty-six at 112 lbs, four hundred and thirteen at 20 lbs, plus fifty baby incendiaries. Eleven thousand two hundred and thirty one rounds of small arms ammunition were fired from the Lewis Guns. A full report of the effect of this attack was published a few days later and it indicates that, "Good results were obtained, but targets in the shape of personnel and flocks were non existent". These operations, chiefly against the tribe of GURI KHEL continued until, at the end of October, the tribe capitulated and decided to comply with the terms offered.

It is of interest to note that at the same time, many experiments were being made to improve the efficiency of the Squadron in its army co-operation work. For example the location and indication of unseen points was tried by using W/T from an aeroplane to the ground, whilst another machine successfully indicated the positions by first flying over them, and then zooming eight times in their direction.

The average flying hours over this period were two hundred per month and when not engaged in operations, this time was spent in training exercises.

March 1924 found the Squadron at AMBALA, the move from DARDONI being completed by the 13th of this month. The flight was accomplished as follows:- "One flight, with extra tanks, went straight through to LAHORE, a distance of 270 miles. The other two flights broke their journey at MIANWALI to fill up. On the 13th March all twelve machines flew in Squadron formation from LAHORE to AMBALA, arriving without a hitch".

It was during 1924 that several long distance flights were made by aeroplanes of various countries. In April two of the Squadrons' Pilots, Flying Officer WALSER and Flying Officer COOMBE, flew to AGRA to meet a French aviator Lt. Pelletier D'OISY in his flight across India. They remained there several days, seeing the French machine off again before returning to AMBALA on the 5th. They had waited in the hope of meeting two Portuguese flyers, Captain SAREMENTO BIERES and Captain BRITO PAES, who were attempting a flight to MACAO, the Portuguese colony near to HONG KONG. The Portuguese machine had, unfortunately forced landed, or crashed in JODHPUR STATE before reaching AGRA. The Squadron did, however, meet these two pilots as they passed through AMBALA on the 30th April, having obtained a new D.H.9A from the Royal Air Force.

In June, practice night bombing was commenced and good results were obtained dropping from 1000 feet on a target consisting of a bunch of flares on the aerodrome. Further night bombing practices were carried out and in April 1925, a flight was detached to TANK solely for the purpose of night bombing operations. On the 1st April the first successful night bombing raid was carried out and considerable damage caused to caves and cultivation. It was stated at this time that "night flying was reported to have caused considerable consternation amongst the hostiles".

In the meantime, in addition to normal service training, other interesting flights were made. On 19th July experiments were made in "collecting messages by means of chasing and catching hydrogen balloons". Starting at the beginning of November Flying Officer COOMBE carried out a survey flight over a distance of approximately 1,000 miles. In March 1925, "members of the Legislative Council were taken up for flights from DELHI, and appeared extremely gratified at their experiences".

On the 16th April, after a final night raid, the detachment at TANK was recalled "owing to the light becoming too bad for a continuation of night flying arrangements". Though the detachment had been of a short duration the technique of night bombing had been improved. In the final attacks parachute flares were used and "the bombing aeroplanes gained maximum height over TANK aerodrome and then approached the targets with engines throttled back".

Normal routine was continued throughout the year, but a flight worthy of note was made in conjunction with the first arrival between QUETTA and SIMLA. "A Bristol Fighter, of No. 31 Squadron, fitted with three petrol tanks left QUETTA at 06.00 hours on Wednesday, 16th September, 1925, flying direct to DIERA ISMAIL KHAN. Here a D.H.9A was waiting to take the mail on, and the change-over was effected at 09.15 hrs. The D.H.9A flew direct to LAHORE arriving there at 11.40 hrs, handing the mail over to another Bristol Fighter. An unavoidable delay of 45 minutes was experienced here due to a severe dust storm, the third aeroplane being unable to proceed until 12.25 hrs. SIMLA was reached at 15.05 hrs, the mail being accurately dropped in the usual message bags. The aeroplane then returned to AMBALA but had to make a forced landing on the way, unfortunately in very difficult country. The machine was damaged but happily the pilot and passenger were unhurt. This was the first time that airmail had been attempted between QUETTA and SIMLA and the mail was actually delivered eight hours and forty-five minutes after leaving QUETTA, an answer being despatched to QUETTA by wireless within an hour of its receipt. By normal methods of transport it would have taken three or four days, and the trial was considered a great success.

In March 1926 an aeroplane proceeded to MEERUT in order to take part in a torchlight tattoo. At 21.35 hrs. on the 4th March it took off and climbed to 6,000 feet where it was picked out by four searchlights. The machine was carrying a battery of five Verey pistols on a Scarfe mounting and its tail and fuselage were illuminated by small lamps. After a display of Pyrotechnics, Aerobatics were executed before a landing was made by the use of wing tips flares.

A Flight was attached to QUETTA during May, and for the remainder of the year the Squadron applied itself to intensive training, army co-operation practices and experimental flying, averaging 250 to 300 hours per month. Typical flying training consisted of formation practice including driving in formation: attacking a pre-arranged target in succession and reforming; night cloud and compass course flying, forced landing practices; message picking up front and rear camera gun and Popham panel practices; puff shoots; W/T and tests, photography and reconnaissances; with sketches.

On the experimental side altitude tests were made in July. The aeroplane carrying a full load reached 11,300 feet in one hour and thirty five minutes. A successful test was also carried out using the Gosport speaking tubes, the ear pieces being fitted with rubber sponges to minimise noise.

1 9 2 7

The intensive formation flying training, resulted in the Squadron acquitting itself extremely well in an air display which was held in Delhi on the 21st February, 1927. During this display it was engaged in the relay

air race and formation flying by R/T. The show ended with a formation fly
past.

In December, eleven aircraft escorted HIS MAJESTY the KING of
AFGHANISTAN on his arrival at, and departure from CHAMAN and QUETTA. One
of the machines force landed in the CHAMAN area owing to the pilot losing
his way in the clouds, and both he and his observer were taken prisoner.
They spent several days in captivity before they were released unharmed on
the 12th of the month.

1928

At the beginning of 1928 a significant step was taken, in that
experiments were made during January in the dropping of supplies from the air.
It was in this role that some of the Squadrons most stirring exploits took
place in World War II. The containers were apparently slung below the main-
plane and parachuted down from a height of 500 ft., whilst the aircraft was
flown at an airspeed of 90 to 110 miles per hour. In October an opportunity
came to enable these supply dropping trials and experiments to be put to the
test when a patrol of armoured cars and lorries became stranded on the TOBA
plateau, owing to a breakdown of one of the vehicles. Head Quarters Western
Command, anxious as to the position of this convoy, requested that aircraft
should endeavour to locate it. The convoy was duly found, supplies were
dropped, messages were picked up, and it was maintained generally from the
air for several days before it was able to proceed.

QUETTA had been the Squadron's base for several years and was to
remain so until the disastrous earthquake in 1935. There were several attach-
ments to FORT SANDEMAN coincident with sporadic tribal uprisings but in the
main its activities consisted of general service training and army co-operation
practices, the latter again necessitating several detachments.

1929

During September, 1929 very serious flooding resulted in parts of the
road between QUETTA and KARACHI being washed away. This caused a temporary
suspension of the mail service and two of the Squadron's aircraft were used
to carry mails. A similar incident occurred in 1930 when floods breached
the railway line between JACOBABAD and RETIF, this time the whole Squadron
was engaged, in time, for a period of thirty three days, operating from
JACOBABAD. In all 304 sorties, resulting in three hundred and eighty-seven
hours being flown carried a load of 94,355 lbs. of mail.

1931

The first Warspite Mark IIA aeroplane with Jupiter VIIIF engine was
received on the 20th February, 1931. By the 13th June the Squadron was

completely equipped with this type and the faithful Bristol Fighters moved into retirement.

1 9 3 3

On the 2nd March, 1933 a notable test was made to ascertain the length of time taken to photograph an operational area, return to the unit, develop, print and deliver the photographs. The task was accomplished in several hours from the time that the details were received in the Flight Office to the delivery of fifty-four prints to the Army.

It was also during this year that the Sir Geoffrey Salmon Bombing Cup for any co-operation Squadrons was won. The same trophy was again held by the Squadron in 1935 when the average bombing error was 97.9 yards.

1 9 3 5

At approximately 03.00 hrs. on the 31st May, 1935 a severe earthquake took place at QUETTA causing serious damage to life and property. The Royal Air Force suffered some 160 casualties of which approximately 52 were killed, as the earthquake destroyed practically every building on the station. The barrack blocks were completely destroyed, the majority of the airmen being buried under the debris. The Squadron's casualties in personnel consisted of twenty-two airmen and many of the aircraft were damaged.

However, rescue and repair work continued throughout the day and eventually three machines were airborne to ascertain the extent of the earthquake area and to establish communications with SIMLA. The next few days were spent in salvage, repair and re-organisation and all personnel were accommodated under canvas until the 2nd June, when they were moved up to the lines of the 1st Batt. Queens Royal Regiment. On that day another severe shock occurred at 15.10 hours, but by the 3rd June all the aeroplanes were serviceable, and the evacuation of the Squadron to DRIGH ROAD KARACHI was completed by the 8th June.

On the 7th July HIS EXCELLENCY the Viceroy of INDIA inspected and addressed the Squadron as follows:-

"Wing Commander Slessor, Officers and Airmen of No.3 (India) Wing.

I am very glad to have this opportunity today of paying my tribute to you all in my position as Governor General of India, for the way in which you faced your recent terrible experiences in QUETTA.
I deplore very deeply the heavy casualties suffered by No.3 (India) Wing of the Royal Air Force and I sympathise with you sincerely in the loss of your comrades.
Notwithstanding the nerve shattering experiences in which your branch of the Service suffered more heavily than any other,

the way in which you met and overcame the effects of the catastrophe was magnificent. I have been told of the rapidity with which you set to work to extricate your comrades from the ruins of your quarters and subsequently to save property from the wreckage.

The speed with which you got your damaged aircraft into action again was remarkable and proved of the greatest value.

The Government of India are truly grateful for the splendid service which the aircraft in QUETTA gave in reporting the conditions of outlying districts immediately after the earthquake in flying emergency requirements to QUETTA and in evacuating casualties.

Let me express to you all in conclusion my admiration of the fine spirit you have displayed throughout the disaster, and warmly congratulate you on maintaining to the full that spirit of courage and initiative which has always been a tradition of your service."

The following Squadron Officers were presented to HIS EXCELLENCY the Viceroy.

Sqn.Ldr. Macfarlane and Flt.Lt. Huxham.

It was not until the 14th August that the Squadron was able to return to its pre-earthquake activities, and even then a limited flying programme only was possible. The Squadron, in effect, had had to be reformed, and the equipment at this time consisted of two flights of Warspite (Jupiter 8F.B's) only.

As time progressed the Squadron reached full strength again and its normal training and army co-operation duties were resumed until 1937 when the most serious Waziristan disturbances for some considerable time occurred. Although no part was played in the quelling of these a flight was detailed to FORT SANDEMAN as it was thought that tribesmen in that area might join battle in sympathy. This proved to be a wrong assumption and no offensive action was necessary, although many reconnaissances were flown. In the meantime photographic survey played a large part in the Squadron activities and many areas were photographed for subsequent mapping by the army.

Similar work continued until the middle of 1939 when in August of that year it was decided to convert the Squadron to a bomber transport formation. Valencia aircraft of 216 Squadron MELIOPOLIS were available for the re-equipment and some were flown by Squadron crews from ALEXNADRIA to INDIA whilst the remainder of the aircraft arrived crated and were assembled at the Air Depot, KARACHI.

After re-equipping the Squadron moved to LAHORE and absorbed the bomber transport flight, which had been in existence there since 1929. Later in the year a further move was made to PESHEWAR, from where many bombing raids were carried out in North West Frontier operations. During the course of these attacks several direct hits were scored on the cave of the FAQUIR of IPI. These operations continued throughout 1940 and during this year a complete CHITRAL RELIEF was carried out by air. This was thought to be an important event, as it is believed that this was the first and only occasion that the relief was carried out by this method.

1 9 4 1

In February 1941, the entire Squadron was mustered to move the ground personnel of two other Squadrons to the Far East consequent upon the threat of Japan to join in the war on the side of the Axis powers. This task was carried out between the 8th and the 14th February. A Flight transporting No.27 personnel to SINGAPORE and B Flight transporting No.60 Squadron's personnel to RANGOON. In the meantime the Squadron H.Q. moved to LAHORE to which location both flights returned at the beginning of March. On the 26th March with the threat of rebellion brewing in IRAQ, the entire Squadron moved to KARACHI.

From KARACHI A and B Flights, commanded by Squadron Leader BURNSIDE D.F.C. and Squadron Leader BURBURY, respectively, carried out two return flights to SHAIBAH between the 2nd and 9th of April carrying personnel of the 2nd Battalion Kings Regiment. The route followed was KARACHI-JIWANI-SHARJAH (night stop) - BAHREIN - SHAIBAH, and the average flying time per crew over the eight days was 92 hours.

The period 12th to 15th April was spent in converting B Flight to Douglas D.C.2 aircraft and on the 16th both Flights, that is A Flight still with Valencias and B Flight with four D.C.2's carried further reinforcements to SHAIBAH where they remained as a detachment, four more D.C.2's being taken over from civil pilots there.

On the 18th April whilst flying reinforcements from SHAIBAH to HABBANIYA a Valencia piloted by Sgt. CHALK landed on K4 landing ground and the crew members together with fifteen men of the Kings Regiment were taken prisoners by the Iraquis. It seems that a skirmish occurred during which the second pilot Sgt. FARR was wounded and the Valencia burnt out. A second Valencia landed at the same airfield but managed to take off again, though not before two members of the crew had been wounded by light machine gun fire.

The detachment moved to BASRAH on the 19th April and continued to fly men, stores and equipment to HABBANIYA daily. About the 29th April the Germans began using ME.110's and HE.111's based on HINAIDI and MOSUL as all flying had to be carried out at night. During this period many evacuees and casualties were flown out of HABBANIYA.

The ferrying of men and material was continued throughout the month of May, although one D.C.2 was knocked out during a strafe of HABBANIYA by ME.110's. The detachment carried out over 18.00 hrs. of flying during the month using six Valencias and six D.C.2's. The ground crews put up a most magnificent show working all hours of the day and night under the most difficult conditions and in great heat. The Valencias in particular were extremely difficult to maintain and all major inspections were dispensed with.

On the 1st June the detachment, now commanded by Wing Commander UBEE, A.F.C., moved to HABBANIYA and commenced to operate in the SYRIAN theatre of war throughout June and July. Its principal task was the evacuation of casualties, and many trips were made to the Middle East.

In August B Flight returned to KARACHI whilst A Flight moved to SHAIBAH to take part in operations against IRAN. During these operations two Valencias were lost but there were no casualties.

September found the whole Squadron back in INDIA operating long distance flights from LAHORE, many carrying Very Important Persons, one of whom was General Sir Archibald Wavell, Commander in Chief INDIA.

The Squadron was not to remain together for long however, as in late October eight D.C.2's led by Wing Commander Jenkins, the new officer commanding, proceeded on attachment to the MIDDLE EAST air forces. This detachment was based at BILBAIS in the Canal Zone and many sorties were made into the Western Desert carrying supplies and evacuating casualties. One D.C.2 piloted by W/O Lord was shot down by three ME.110's. The pilot crash landed successfully but Howell his second pilot was wounded and one passenger was killed. It is of interest to note here that this same pilot, W/O Lord, who was later commissioned and awarded the D.F.C. for his exploits in BURMA whilst still serving with the Squadron, was to become Transport Commands only V.C. the award of which was made posthumously for his gallantry over ARNHEM, whilst serving with 271 Squadron.

Many flights were also made to CYPRUS by this detachment and on one occasion a journey to STALINGRAD and back was made.

The outbreak of hostilities against JAPAN in December found the Indian Command lamentably short of transport aircraft, for with the detachment operating in the Middle East only two serviceable D.C.2's remained with the Squadron at LAHORE and these were the only two transport aircraft in the command. These aircraft were sent to fly between RANGOON and CALCUTTA carrying urgent stores and evacuating personnel until ultimately one was destroyed during a JAPANESE air raid on MINGALADON AIRFIELD.

At the beginning of February 1942 the Middle East detachment returned and the whole Squadron was located at AKYAB. From this base, off the ARAKAN Coast, reinforcements were flown into BURMA and sick and wounded were evacuated on the return trips. These operations continued until the end of March, when the Squadron was forced to move back to CALCUTTA after enemy action had rendered AKYAB untenable.

Up to mid April operations were continued from DUM DUM, Calcutta, carrying reinforcements into MAGWE, SCHWEBO, and MYITKYINA in turn as the battle moved northwards. Sick and wounded were also evacuated from these places, and when there were no casualties to move, civilians were brought out. One "escape ship" flew every evening to AKYAB at dusk until the port finally fell into Japanese hands. An aircraft was lost on one of the last sorties of this nature, through running into an unfilled bomb crater. Although the aircraft was a write-off the valuable engines were salvaged.

1 9 4 2

All aircraft by this time were in very poor shape. When the Squadron first took them over airframe hours varied between 8,000 and 17,000 and engine hours between 2,000 and 10,000. Owing to the emergency and the acute shortage of transport aircraft, major inspections were overlooked and each aircraft was flown six to ten hours daily. Taking all this into account, together with the shortage of spares and the complete lack of spare engines, it is remarkable that the aircraft were kept flying. It speaks very highly of the efforts of the Squadron's maintenance personnel. By the end of March the total number of aircraft on Squadron strength amounted to eight D.C.2's only.

About the middle of April the first D.C.3 aircraft arrived and by the 20th of the month three of these aircraft were on Squadron strength. The situation in Central Burma was at the time precarious and it was decided to send a detachment to DINJAN to operate from that base to MYITKYINA in Central Burma. The three D.C.3's and one D.C.2 formed the detachment and the remainder of the Squadron returned to LAHORE with the D.C.2's which by now were in need of a complete overhaul. The detachment flew in and out of MYITKYINA until its fall on the 8th May after which there were no airfields left to the allies in BURMA.

On the 6th May whilst two aircraft were on the ground at MYITKYINA enemy aircraft were heard overhead. It was decided to continue loading and then take off as quickly as possible as it was believed that the aircraft was only a reconnaissance plane. As one aircraft was about to take off and the other taxi-ing out, bombs fell destroying the port wing of the first aircraft causing it to swing right round and crash. The starboard engine and tyre of the second aircraft were also damaged. A few seconds later low flying machine gun attacks were made on the aircraft and landing strip, and these continued for some ten minutes. In the meantime the crews had abandoned their aircraft and it is believed that Squadron Leader HOWELS, one of the pilots, severely damaged the Japanese aircraft by fire from his Tommy Gun during its last attack and that it crashed or forced landed in a nearby river bed. This however, was not confirmed.

Immediately the attacks ceased first aid was given to the injured. Apart from casualties amongst a crowd of evacuees, two women passengers and a child had been killed, whilst two army doctors had been seriously wounded. Fortunately it was found that the runway was still usable and the two other D.C.3's arrived, loaded and departed without trouble, though the strip was subjected to further attacks throughout the day. All Royal Air Force personnel were evacuated in the evening. By 8th May the strip was in Japanese hands and no further evacuations were possible.

After MYITKYINA had fallen the only allied outpost which remained in BURMA was a remote and isolated garrison at FORT HERTZ. This consisted of a small party of British personnel including some women, who had reached this point after the Japanese had pushed northwards through BURMA. They were without food, money, arms or spare clothing and the only means of maintaining them was by air. It was here that supply dropping in Burma had its modest beginning, when the Squadron first dropped supplies at FORT HERTZ on the 9th May. This means of supply continued throughout the month until it was decided that a determined effort should be made to evacuate the party by air. To this end several sorties were mounted by the Squadron in early June, but they were frustrated by bad weather. On the 13th June, however, the weather conditions cleared sufficiently to enable an aircraft of the Squadron to reach FORT HERTZ, where landing and taking off in an extremely confined space it successfully evacuated 23 persons.

By now the Americans were making regular flights across the "HUMP" from India to China, and Indian Command decided that FORT HERTZ should be developed into an emergency landing ground and outpost, along this route. By the 24th August a landing ground had been prepared there and on the next day the first of many landings was made by one of the Squadron's aircraft. Up to the 10th September a total of 197 persons together with necessary equipment had been transported to FORT HERTZ by air. Thereafter the Garrison was entirely dependent upon air supply, carried out by the Squadron's detachment at DINJAN.

During June of 1942 the first two Dakotas, especially designed for troop carrying and supply dropping, were received by the Squadron and soon put into commission. FORT HERTZ was not the only place receiving attention from the Squadron's aircraft during the year. Many other evacuee columns were also air supplied, for instance, on the 19th July, a sortie was made to HKALAK GA and, besides stores, ten packets each containing 500 rupees in old currency silver were dropped. This money was used to obtain the co-operation of native tribesmen in aiding a relief party to establish a receiving centre there for Chinese troops and evacuees. Information was later received from a senior army officer that "the pilot who dropped the money at HKALAK GA on the 19th July did some good shooting - nine packets out of ten were collected, though they bounced hundreds of feet into the jungle. A further detachment was operated from TEZPUR during the year and many air supply sorties were made from there.

At the beginning of 1943 whilst the Japanese Air Force was engaged in tactical operations against our forces in the ARAKAN, the first WINGATE expedition was launched into North Burma. Wingate went forth from IMPHAL in February, seemingly in an antique way with pack mules and bullock carts, but taking with him R.A. Liaison Officers and radio apparatus, so that each column could call for air aid and supplies when needed. During the months of March and April the expedition was maintained behind the enemy lines by Dakotas of the 31st Squadron, which had now moved to AGATARLA, assisted by Hudsons of 194 Squadron. It was during this operation that the Squadron, for the first time, dropped supplies by night, as well as by day. At first fighter escorts had been provided but when the bulk of the infantry were beyond the river CHINDWIN, approaching the MYITKYINA railway, this was impossible owing to the limited range of the fighters. After the conclusion of the operation Wingate stated that he "considered these supply dropping operations a brilliant and unexpected success", and reports from other personnel in the field indicated the same.

1943

In addition to the Wingate expedition the Squadron's commitments were many and included a continuous heavy airlift for the army units in the CHIN HILLS and the maintainance of SUMPRABUM and FORT HERTZ.

During the early part of this year all of the obsolete D.C.2's and
D.C.3's were replaced by Dakotas and this resulted in an appreciable increase
in pay loads carried and a consequent increase in the amount of supplies
dropped and transported. In spite of the 1943 monsoon weather and the
formidable difficulties which the ground staffs had to overcome the number
of supply droppings sorties flown by the Squadron reached the record figure
in June of 286 during which eighty four tons of supplies were dropped. This
tempo was maintained by the Squadron's aircraft operating from AGATRARLA for
the supply of the CHIN HILLS and ARAKAN, and from DINJAN for North Burma.
The average serviceability throughout this period amounted to only ten Dokatas
per day. At the end of the rainy season the G.O.C. in C Eastern Army expressed
the view that "without the maintenance of supply from the air, the army could
not have held throughout the monsoon, the positions in which it had entrenched
itself at the end of the campaigning season in May". He added that "owing to
the efforts of No.31 Squadron none of the troops have ever gone hungry and many
friendly inhabitants of distant tracts had been saved from great hardship".

The opening of the new campaigning season in the Autumn of 1943 found
the Squadron fulfilling its routine supply dropping commitments in the areas
of FORT HERTZ and the CHIN HILLS, much as it had been doing throughout the
previous twelve months. In addition several flights over the "Hump" to KUNMING
were made each month. Very soon, however, further transport Squadrons reinforce
the Command and the scope of transport operations broadened considerably.

1943 - 1944

On the 4th February 1944 the Japanese launched an offensive in the
ARAKAN and succeeded in cutting off the 7th Division. According to all
precedents from the Malayan campaign onwards the Allied Forces, deeply
embarrassed by the severance of their communications, should have hastily
abandoned their fortified positions and beaten a retreat towards their base.
In fact, nothing of the sort occurred. The reinforcements of the enemy had
been observed and arrangements had already been made for air supply when the
offensive developed. No.31 Squadron combining with the other Squadrons of
the Transport force now available carried out the air supply of the isolated
7th Division with great skill and courage. Not only basic supplies were
dropped, but also the new South East Asia Command newspaper, cigarettes and
mail from home. The despatch of these amenities had a great morale effect
upon the troops who realized that their predicament was temporary and by no
means hopeless.

At this time the enemy made determined efforts, both from the air and
from the ground to impede the air supply operations, and eventually in the
face of this, the times of dropping were transferred to darkness.

Scarcely had the struggle in the ARAKAN subsided when a conflict on
a larger scale flared up in the north, where General STILLWELL's forces were
trying to reopen the land route to CHINA from the west. It was in conjunction
with this campaign that Wingate's second expedition came into being. Again,
for long periods the operation depended entirely upon air supply. The
Squadron operated in all phases of the expedition from the initial landings

behind the enemy to the supply of the troops by parachutes. Much depended upon the accuracy of these parachute drops since the Dropping Zones were small and they were constantly being changed as the columns moved from place to place. Moreover, dropping normally took place at night and there was often no other guide than the Navigator's skill, supplemented by pre-arranged light signals which became visible only when the aircraft arrived in the vicinity of the Dropping Zones.

With the onset of the rains in the second half of May, the Squadron's dropping commitments to Wingate's expedition dwindled, though they continued in a small scale throughout the monsoon during which night dropping ceased. Day dropping escorted by Mustang fighters encountered no enemy opposition. The standards of dropping achieved during this operation was high and as a result a fine co-operative spirit developed between the Army and the Royal Air Force.

Meanwhile on the Central Front the Japanese were laying siege to IMPHAL and a tactical situation, similar to that of the ARAKAN struggle developed, except that the forces involved were much larger. The IMPHAL plain extends well over a thousand square miles and on it the IV Corps, comprising of 4 divisions together with 221 group R.A.F. were besieged. During this siege which lasted three months the Squadron was kept extremely busy along with its sister Squadrons, carrying innumerable varieties of loads to isolated areas. In fact, it may well be that the phrase " ubiquitous " was derived from this large variety of loads carried. During April, for instance, an analysis of the Squadron's statistics reads:-

Hours Flown	1908.
Supplies Dropped	1,471,400 lbs.
Freight Transported	427,400 lbs.
Men Transported	983.
Mules Transported	103.
Horses Transported	3.
Bullocks Transported	4.

Plus 2 Bofers Guns, 1 Jeep, and 1 Motor cycle.

In July of 1944 the Squadron moved back to BASAL for a well-earned rest period. During the six months prior to its withdrawal from the base at AGATARLA in BENGAL, a total of 13,200 hours had been flown on operations for a loss of six aircraft. The stay at BASAL was short, but long enough to train new crews in dropping technique and to give the whole Squadron practice in night cross countries, in formation, paratroop dropping and glider towing. December found them back at AGATARLA and back on operational supply dropping - 108,700 lbs being dropped on the 2nd December in the TIDDIM area. The Squadron continued to give close support to the rapidly advancing 14th Army units and morale was very high, until a peak was reached during the month of April. Operating from HATHAZARI record breaking totals of supplies dropped and loaded to the 14th Army during its victorious march from MEKTALA to RANGOON, were reached and 3,938 operational hours were flown during the month. The aircrews were flying from 8 to 12 hours every alternate day through rapidly deteriorating pre-monsoon weather conditions. Most of the loads consisted of army rations, stores, etc., and a large amount of ammunition. The two main areas of dropping and loading operations were MEKTALA and MYITCHE in Central

Burma. During a period when MEKTALA was entirely cut off from land communication the Squadron's aircraft moved in a complete Casualty Clearing Station, from INDAINGLALE. This was all achieved with an average daily serviceability of sixteen aircraft.

In June the Squadron moved to KYAUKPU on RAMREE Island and though RANGOON had fallen in May the lack of harbour and rail facilities and the effect of the monsoon rains upon the dirt roads made it imperative that air transport should still be used. These reasons, combined with the fact that our troops were concerned with consolidating and supplying their positions along the TOUNGOO-PEGU Railway and were also engaging the Japanese forces in fierce battles as they tried to withdraw, allowed no let up in the commitments of the Squadron. During the month 3,400 hours were flown mainly on air landing operations. The object of most of the sorties being to land men and materials on strips in the Central Plains of Burma, and eventually these trips were termed "Milk Runs" by the crews. The same type of operations were flown during July, though there were several detachments to various places. A few aircraft were detached to TOUNGOO and it was their task to supply guerrilla fighters of FORCE 136 throughout the length of the SHAW HILLS. The weather throughout this period was typical solid monsoon rain, continuous for three weeks with never a break of more than one hour.

During the month of August the Squadron started to move to TILDA in the Central Provinces of India, there to train and prepare for glider and paratroop operations which were to open the way to the recapture of SINGAPORE. Towards the 12th August the move was well under way when rumour was heard that Japan had asked for peace terms and soon this became official. This of course meant that training programmes would be cancelled and for a short while no one seemed to know whether the Squadron was to continue to TILDA or remain at RAMREE. Finally, an order was received to proceed to MINGALADON (RANGOON) but no sooner had the advance party been sent than this was altered to AKYAB, where eventually after much chaos the Squadron found itself.

From now on it was engaged in the speeding up of the rescue and repatriation of Allied prisoners of war and internees. During September another move was made to KALLANG, Singapore from where many sorties were made carrying essential supplies to, and P.O.W's from many camps in Malaya and Dutch East Indies. In October what was probably the most unique consignment ever assigned to a 31st Squadron, if not R.A.F. Crew was transported. Seventy-two "Chinese Comfort Girls" were flown from MEDAN to PEWANG. They had been found by the authorities in a brothel at MEDAN, where they had been forcibly employed by the Japanese as "Welfare Facilities" having been brought over from PEWANG for this purpose. Also during this month a detachment was sent to BATAVIA and this was strengthened during November and prepared to take part in large scale operations. This detachment was necessary because there were indications that Indonesian extremists were preparing to "Declare War" on the British forces in JAVA. A state of war did in fact rapidly develop and a Squadron aircraft crashed on the 15th November after being fired upon by a Bofors Gun whilst actually on the circuit, preparing to land at SOERABAYA.

A most regrettable and shocking incident occurred on the 28th November when another of the Squadron's aircraft crashed near to BATAVIA. From the air

it was seen that the crew and passengers had survived the forced landing.
A party proceeded to the scene by road to pick up the survivors only to find
them missing. It was assumed that they had set off themselves for the airfield
on foot. Contrary to expectations they did not arrive at Headquarters and a
further search was made by the army, the Indonesians being unco-operative and
hostile. It was subsequently discovered that the crew and passengers had been
foully butchered by about fifty Indonesian soldiers after having spent the
night in the jail of their barracks. No message was found on the walls of
their cells, possibly because eye witnesses reported that they had been
severely beaten up before being massacred.

1 9 4 6

By January the whole Squadron was at KEMAJUNAN (BATAVIA) where
conditions were much quieter than previously and personnel were able to walk
around in daylight with only the remotest chance of getting shot. Its main
task was supplying BAWDOENG with food and materials and the aircrews were
making several sorties per day on this "Bus Run".

On the 5th February the following signal was received from the A.O.C.
in C., S.E.A.A.F.

"Number 31 Squadron has completed no less than 39 sorties a day.
These sorties have included the transporting of troops, R.A.W.P.I. medical
stores and supplies between various points in JAVA, SUMATRA and SINGAPORE.

2.   The conditions under which No. 31 Squadron operated are without doubt
the most arduous in South East Asia. They are working, in fact, under active
service conditions over hostile country.

3.   Despite these factors they have surmounted all the difficulties and
have emerged triumphant, keeping up the traditions of the Royal Air Force in
the best way possible.

4.   I thank the aircrews and ground staffs of No. 31 Squadron for their
splendid work".

Supply dropping was carried out to an ambushed convoy of 37th Brigade
during March and this resulted in the following message being received by the
Squadron:- "Many thanks all ranks of 37th Brigade for splendid and consistent
drops during March. Daily prayer from men gazing skywards. Quote: 'Send it
down David' Unquote: Good Luck".

During July, after many months of close support activity scheduled
runs were carried out for a month. The aircrews found them a pleasant change
and they speedily adapted themselves to the finer points of airline passenger
carrying. When this work ceased, close support of operations in Indonesia
continued until the Squadron was disbanded at BATAVIA on the 30th September,
to be reformed at MAURIPUR (KARACHI) in November of the same year. For a
time scheduled route flying was carried out from MAURIPUR to such places as
JIWANI, SANTA CRUZ, BANGALORE, CHAKLALA, CAWNPORE, etc., much the same type
of work in fact that the Squadron had been carrying out in 1939 when it was
last stationed at KARACHI.

1 9 4 7

At the beginning of 1947 a detachment was based at MOHANBARI in Assam and engaged upon food relief dropping missions. The main tasks of the Squadron until the partition of India and its independence consisted of scheduled flights, special flights, continuation training and supply drops, with a spell of paratroop refresher training at CHAKLALA.

September saw the start of the withdrawal of R.A.F. units from India and Pakistan and in consequence the Squadron moved to PALAM (Delhi) from whence it detached twelve aircraft on the 12th to CHAKLALA for the purpose of refugee evacuation. It assisted in the centralisation of many of the R.A.F. units spread over the country until it eventually returned to MAURIPUR in November. A brief period of scheduled services to JIWANI and mail runs preceded its disbandment on 31st December, 1947.

1 9 4 8

The Squadron was not reformed again until 13th August, 1948 when the Metropolitan Communication Squadron, which had been operating from HENDON for a number of years assumed the No. 31 Squadron. This was the first time that the Squadron had been in England since its formation in 1915. Equipped with light communication aircraft such as PROCTORS, ANSONS and latterly DEVONS it has served a unique role to the present day. Not only does it afford opportunities to officers serving at Air Ministry to keep in flying practice, but it enables such officers to proceed on staff visits to anywhere in the U.K. or on the continent by air, flying themselves. When this is not possible the Squadron provides fully qualified crews for such purposes. Many V.I.P's are also carried by the Squadron's crews and aircraft. Furthermore the Squadron provides two Ambulance Aircraft at continuous stand-by and operation. It is interesting to note that when an emergency call was made by Glasgow Health Authorities for vaccine during the Smallpox Epidemic in 1950, 31st Squadron at 10 minutes notice flew this vaccine to Scotland. -

The Squadron duties and tradition continue........

LIST OF SQUADRON COMMANDERS. 31st SQUADRON.

CAPT. C.Y. MacDONALD	11.10.15.
MAJOR C.R.S. BRADLEY	27. 3.16.
MAJOR S. HUTCHESON	23. 5.17.
MAJOR R.G.H. MURRAY, M.C.	22. 7.17.
MAJOR E.L. MILLAR, M.B.E.	1.12.18.
FL/LT D.H.M. CARBERRY, M.C.,D.F.C.	10. 8.19.
SQN/LDR A.L. NEALE, M.C.	22. 1.20.
SQN/LDR A.T. HARRIS, A.F.C.	26. 1.21.
SQN/LDR A.C. MAUND, C.B.E.,D.S.O.	6. 5.22.
SQN/LDR A.A. WALSER, M.C.,D.F.C.	2. 5.24.
SQN/LDR H.S. POWELL, M.C.	20. 6.24.
SQN/LDR J.O. ARCHER, C.B.E.	18.11.25.
SQN/LDR J.F. GORDON, D.F.C.	31. 4.26.
SQN/LDR BURTON ANKERS, D.C.M.	25. 3.31.
SQN/LDR C.J.S. DEARLOVE	15. 2.34.
SQN/LDR R.M.C. MacFARLANE	21.11.34.
SQN/LDR J.L. AIREY	19.10.35.
SQN/LDR A.V. HAMMOND	21. 6.37.
SQN/LDR F.F. WICKS, D.F.C.	9.10.38.
WG/CDR REID, A.F.C.	1939.
WG/CDR NICHOLLS	12.40.
WG/CDR S.E. UBEE, A.F.C.	1. 6.41.
WG/CDR H.P. JENKINS	10.41.
WG/CDR W.H. BURBURY, D.F.C.,A.F.C.	1. 6.42.
WG/CDR H.A. OLIVIER	30. 5.43.
WG/CDR W.H. BURBURY, D.F.C.,A.F.C.	14. 1.44.
WG/CDR R.O. ALTMAN, D.F.C.	2. 2.45.
WG/CDR B.R. MacNAMARA, D.S.O.	
WG/CDR T.W. GILLAN (SICK))	21. 7.46.
SQN/LDR D.W.S. EVANS)	
WG/CDR J.M. COOKE, D.S.O.,D.F.C.	1.11.46.
WG/CDR C. FOTHERGILL	15. 9.47.
WG/CDR A.R. FANE DE SALIS	19. 7.48.
WG/CDR R.E. RIDGWAY, D.S.O.	10. 3.50.

Ranks and decorations are those held at date of appointment.

LOCATIONS

"A" FLIGHT	FARNBOROUGH	ENGLAND	11.10.15.
	NOWSHERA	INDIA	26.12.15.
	RISALPUR	INDIA	1. 3.16.
	MURREE	INDIA	APRIL, 1916.
"B" FLIGHT	GOSPORT	ENGLAND	18. 1.16.
	RISALPUR	INDIA	MARCH, 1916.
	MURREE	INDIA	29. 7.16.
"C" FLIGHT	GOSPORT	ENGLAND	10. 5.16.
	MURREE	INDIA	4. 7.16.

31st SQUADRON RISALPUR   INDIA   5.10.16.
Landing grounds at TANK, BANNU, DERA, ISMAIL KHAN.

MAOW	INDIA	15. 4.20.
CAWNPORE	INDIA	26.11.20.
PESHAWAR	INDIA	19.10.21.
DARDONI	INDIA	17. 4.23.
AMBALA	INDIA	11. 3.24.
QUETTA	INDIA	13.12.26.
KARACHI (Drigh Road)	INDIA	1. 8.35.
KARACHI (Fort Sandeman)	Detach.	1937.
LAHORE	PESHAWAR	1939.
LAHORE - KARACHI - SHAIBAH (detach)		1941.

BASRAH (detach) - HABBANIYA (detach) - LAHORE -
BILBAIS (EGYPT) (detach) - DUMDUM (CALCUTTA) (detach) -
AKYAB DUM-DUM-DINJAN (detach) - LAHORE -

TEZPUR (detach) -	1942.
AGATARLA (BENGAL) - DINJAN (Detach)	1943.

AGATARLA - DINJAN (detach) BASAL (CENTRAL

PROVINCES INDIA) - AGATARLA	1944.
HAHAZARI-RAMREE-TILDA (detach) MINGALADON	1945.

AKYAB-KALLANG (SINGAPORE) - KEMATORAN (BATAVIA)

KEMAJORAN-MAURIPUR (KARACHI)	1946.

MOHANBARI (detach) MAURIPUR-CHAKLALA (detach) -

PALAM (DELHI) - MAURIPUR	1947.
HENDON (ENGLAND)	1948.
